boxing
for
fitness

SAFE AND FUN WORKOUTS TO GET YOU FIGHTING FIT

boxing
for
fitness

SAFE AND FUN WORKOUTS TO GET YOU FIGHTING FIT

CLINTON MCKENZIE & HILARY LISSENDEN

FIREFLY BOOKS

A FIREFLY BOOK

Published by Firefly Books Ltd. 2011

First printing

Publisher Cataloging-in-Publication Data (U.S.)
McKenzie, Clinton.
    Boxing for fitness : safe and fun workouts to get you fighting fit / Clinton McKenzie and Hilary Lissenden.
[192] p. : col. photos. ; cm.
Includes index.
Summary: Describes the techniques involved in boxing, a circuit that includes shadow boxing, skipping, punch bag and focus-pad work. Also explains how a routine can be tailored to address individual fitness goals.
ISBN-13: 978-1-55407-906-3 (pbk.)
    1. Boxing. I. Lissenden, Hilary. II. Title.
796.83 dc22   GV1133.M3546 2011

Library and Archives Canada Cataloguing in Publication
McKenzie, Clinton, 1955-
    Boxing for fitness : safe and fun workouts to get you fighting fit / Clinton McKenzie and Hilary Lissenden.
Includes index.
ISBN 978-1-55407-906-3
    1. Boxing--Training. 2. Physical fitness. I. Lissenden, Hilary II. Title.
GV1137.6.M35 2011   796.83 C2011-900219-1

Published in the United States by
Firefly Books (U.S.) Inc.
P.O. Box 1338, Ellicott Station
Buffalo, New York 14205

Published in Canada by
Firefly Books Ltd.
66 Leek Crescent
Richmond Hill, Ontario L4B 1H

Commissioned by Charlotte Atyeo
Edited by Rebecca Senior
Designed by Greg Stevenson

This book is produced using paper that is made from wood grown in managed, sustainable forests. It is natural, renewable and recyclable. The logging and manufacturing processes conform to the environmental regulations of the country of origin.

Typeset in Meta Plus on 9 on 11pt by Saxon Graphics Ltd, Derby

Printed and bound in China by C&C Offset Printing Co., Ltd

Note
Whilst every effort has been made to ensure that the content of this book is as technically accurate and as sound as possible, neither the author nor the publishers can accept responsibility for any injury or loss sustained as a result of the use of this material.

Photo Credits
Cover photographs © Grant Pritchard; © Shutterstock
Photographs on pages 10, 13, 16, 34, 35, 45, 56, 68, 70, 79, 81, 82, 83, 84, 85, 86, 89, 91, 97, 102, 137, 149, 151, 158, 160, 164 © Shutterstock
Photographs on pages 2, 5, 11, 19, 43 and 105 © Getty Images
All other photographs © Grant Pritchard
Illustrations on pages 9 and 36 © Tom Croft
Illustrations on page 46 © Greg Stevenson

Contents

Acknowledgments

Many people have helped and supported us in bringing this book to fruition. We'd like to thank them all – and to mention especially:

> For giving us the chance, our Publisher, Charlotte Atyeo; and our Editor, Becky Senior.

> For their continued friendship and encouragement, Miriam Bernal, Leigh Bruce, Sally-Ann Cairns, Lee Clayton, Mel Cook, Richard Dix, Tim Dyson, Beckie Lloyd-Jones, Angel McKenzie.

> David Cowland, for his expertise freely given, and all the benefit of his experience.

> Andrew, James and Lindsey at Lemarr Boxing, for providing clothing and gear for the photoshoot.

> Liz Puttick, for having faith in us first.

> The photoshoot models, Adam, Angel, Arbnor, Cat, Christopher, Dave, Duncan, Fausat, Harry, Heather, Leoard, Magda and Rhys.

> Both of our families – they know why.

Preface

Dreams are made of wishes, and wishes do come true. This book represents a dream that has become a reality for me.

Boxing has always been my passion – even as a child, running through the fields of Jamaica in bare feet. I want to thank my dad for encouraging me; he made it all possible. As did all the other people who supported me, throughout my career and ever since.

Those BBC commentaries by Harry Carpenter still linger in my mind. If Harry rated you, then you knew you were good. His voice was the perfect expression of the excitement, the enthusiasm that I myself felt for the sport of boxing. I still do.

Boxing training changed my life. If my words of fitness can change yours, then this book is everything I wanted it to be.

Yours in boxing fitness,

Clinton McKenzie
British & European Champion 1979–89
Olympic quarter-finalist 1976

Foreword

I was delighted to be asked to endorse this book, in which Clinton McKenzie – a much-loved British champion in his day – brings boxing fitness into the light and makes it accessible for everyone to enjoy.

Boxing has been my life, as it has Clinton's, and it's a special kind of world. A fighter needs physical prowess, but other qualities come into play too – both in the gym and in the ring. Things like strategic thinking, self-control and an ability to adapt.

But perhaps the most important lesson to be learned from boxing is something that we in the business call "heart." This is the will to go the distance; the determination to stand up and be counted.

In these pages, Clinton shows us that you don't have to get hit to have heart. You're in safe hands with him, and through your boxing fitness training you will constantly challenge yourself, overcome your physical and mental limitations, and become stronger in every way.

Sir Henry Cooper OBE, KSG
British, Commonwealth and European Heavyweight Champion

Introduction

If you've picked up this book, and are interested in finding out what boxing fitness can do for you, then you're already on the way to putting on a pair of gloves and enjoying a great new kind of workout.

>> What is boxing fitness?

First and foremost, boxing fitness is fun. You get to "make like a boxer" – and let's face it, who hasn't imagined themselves storming up the steps like Rocky, whacking the heavy bag in *Million Dollar Baby*, or polishing up the old "one-two"? With the techniques and training programs described in these pages, you can do it all ... and you can do it without hitting anyone or getting hit back.

> With boxing fitness you will follow almost all the elements involved in a boxer's traditional training regimen. You'll learn how to shadow box, skip, hit the heavy bag, work the speed ball and practice your punching combinations – a routine that develops a unique blend of heart-lung stamina, strength, speed, co-ordination, balance and flexibility.

This training routine places the boxer who is at the top of their game firmly among the fittest athletes in the world. It follows, then, that by training in a similar way, you will quickly see results.

Depending on what you want from your boxing fitness workout, you will lose weight, tone up, get stronger, increase your stamina and improve your performance in other sports and activities. And, perhaps best of all, you will get to "bust" your stress and channel your frustrations in a safe, non-combative environment. (Remember the driver who cut you off on your way to work this morning? Go on – get it all out with your best left hook!)

>> Safety first

What you won't do in the type of training described here is have any glove-to-body contact. This, of course, is the point of the sport of boxing: hitting someone else harder, and more often, than they hit you. It is *not* the point of boxing fitness. By removing the element of bodily contact, boxing fitness also removes the element of risk – so that when you train, only the benefits of the workout remain.

These benefits are entirely achievable by you, no matter what your age, gender, or level of fitness or ability. And because boxing fitness is fun, and really does work, your achievements will motivate you to continue to exercise, to improve and to progress.

>> Is boxing fitness the same as "boxercise"?

The sport of boxing has experienced a dramatic resurgence in popularity over the last few years (see page 7 for a very brief history). This has contributed

Train anywhere with boxing fitness

to the rise of some explosive new workout trends which incorporate boxing moves and techniques into their sessions – boxercise, "boxfit" and "body combat" among them.

Although such developments seem very recent, boxercise and other combat-type training routines have been around since the early 1990s, so that today there is a huge choice of activities available. Usually these are run as group classes, set to music and taught by aerobics and fitness instructors out of recreation centers and health clubs. As their names suggest, they're not an easy option and can really help kick-start your fitness. But boxing fitness as described in these pages is quite a different kind of workout.

So what makes boxing fitness stand out from the rest?

1 The boxing fitness workout **closely mirrors the traditional boxer's regimen**. By following the guidance given in this book, you will have a unique and authentic exercise experience – one that was originally devised (and has been taught for 20 years) by Clinton McKenzie, former boxing champion and professional boxing trainer.

2 While parts of boxing fitness can be taught in a class environment – for example, boxing circuits and shadow boxing – it is essentially an individual workout where **the elements are tailor-made to your own particular goals**. For more information on this, see Part Five, in which we structure a number of different sessions to target specific fitness aspirations and concerns. We also show you how you can still enjoy boxing fitness even if you have limited time, space and/or money available.

3 Boxing fitness is both **flexible and inexpensive**. You don't have to work out at a gym: if you can't get to a registered boxing club, or to one of the many health or fitness gyms that now offer suitable facilities, you can do an adapted version of the workout at home or in the park.

All you need to start is a small initial outlay on a skipping rope, some hand-wraps and possibly some boxing gloves. Do it alone, with a partner, with your personal trainer, or in a group of friends!

> **"**
>
> We meet our boxing instructor in the park after our joint shift, once a week. Training together is fun, and it's also more affordable since we can split the cost between us. Mostly we punch the focus pads, because all three of us love an energetic workout. And the session works well with three people, since we can alternate cardio boxing with core exercises and some basic resistance training – so none of us has to wait around with nothing to do. At the moment, we're working on our bikini bodies!
>
> Magda, Anna and Karolina
> Starbucks baristas **"**

>> How to use this book

To get the best out of your workout, and to ensure that you exercise safely as well as effectively, we advise that you read through this book chronologically. However, if you already possess some knowledge and experience of boxing training, the programs detailed in Part Five can be used as a stand-alone resource.

> **Part One: The Knowledge** gives a brief background to the sport of boxing; sets boxing fitness in its past and present-day context; and details the benefits to you of taking it up.

> **Part Two: The Preparation** comprises all you need to know about how to organize and prepare for your training. We discuss the importance of establishing suitable goals; where, when, how often and for how long to

train; options for exercising with a coach, partner or in a class or group; the importance of hand-wraps and the warm-up; and the equipment and/or facilities you may use to box your way to fitness.

> **Part Three: The Techniques** – the nitty-gritty! Step-by-step, illustrated instructions explain how to stand; how to perform individual punches, combinations, footwork and defensive/evasive techniques; and how to go about all the other elements of boxing fitness, including shadow boxing, skipping, using the punching bag and speed ball, and focus pad work.

> **Part Four: Diet and Health** deals with such matters as good nutrition and hydration; how to prevent common injuries such as sore knuckles – or address them should they unfortunately occur; and some useful precautions to ensure that boxing fitness training can be safely and enjoyably undertaken by those who are older, younger, or less able-bodied.

> **Part Five: The Training Programs** sets out sessions and programs that progress, in clear steps, from complete beginner through to advanced practitioner. There is advice on choosing the right training level; building up your workouts within that level; and determining when it's time to move on to the next phase – together with guidelines on how long that may take.

Alternative techniques and sessions are offered for those who have limited access to facilities and equipment, including our unique boxing circuit, which is designed specifically around the concept of the three-minute round to improve stamina and strengthen all the major muscles involved in boxing training.

> **Part Six: Training Around Your Boxing** talks about core work, resistance training and running – three types of exercise which can greatly enhance your boxing fitness program, even though they don't directly involve boxing techniques. We dispel some of the doubts and

fears surrounding these training techniques, and suggest ways in which they can be incorporated into your sessions for significant fitness gains – no matter what your ability level or goals.

Throughout each section of the book, author, trainer and former boxing champ Clinton McKenzie gets you ahead of the game, providing some invaluable insider info, tips and tricks-of-the-trade. There are checklists to help you achieve the correct technique and avoid common pitfalls, and nuggets of interesting facts about boxing and how it has influenced our popular culture.

Finally, we include real case studies based on the experiences of men, women and young people who have benefited from boxing fitness – featuring direct quotes, practical advice, personal anecdotes and pictures. We hope you'll join them!

PART ONE >> THE KNOWLEDGE

To understand fully what boxing fitness is, and all the ways in which it can benefit you, it helps to know a little about how this type of training evolved – and to dispel a few misconceptions around the sport of boxing, from which boxing fitness has developed. This section shows you how anyone can enjoy boxing fitness, and prepares you for the next step toward starting your training.

What is boxing fitness?

>> A quick word about boxing

The activity we refer to as "boxing" – basically, two people hitting each other – has an ancient history, and has taken many forms in its journey to what we now know as the modern sport.

Stone carvings that date back to at least the third millennium BC depict bare-fisted contests between two individuals, who fought without weapons, gloves or any other kind of protection. Such gruelling encounters endured well into the 19th century, and were termed variously "fisticuffs," "pugilism" or "prizefighting" – because opponents fought for prize money, and spectators bet on the outcome.

Bare-knuckle prizefighting had no rules at all until 1743, when it was determined that you were no longer allowed to strike an opponent when he was "down," nor wrestle or "grapple" him at the waist. At the same time a type of glove, called a "muffler," was designed, but this was used only in training and for exhibitions.

It was not until 1867 that a proper set of rules was introduced to govern this rather dubious pastime, which had by then been outlawed in England and much of the United States. These rules were devised under the patronage of the Marquess of Queensberry, whose name remains associated with them.

There were a total of 12 Queensberry Rules, which specified among other things that fights should be a "fair stand-up boxing match" and conducted in a roped-off ring of 24 square feet or similar. "Rounds"

(boxing intervals) were to be three minutes long, with one minute's rest between each, and padded gloves were to be worn that laced up at the wrist.

From these rules developed boxing as we recognize it today, in both its amateur and professional forms – now strictly controlled by its respective governing bodies, and enforcing stringent safety standards.

FIGHTING TALK

Amateur boxers wear protective headgear, and gloves that have a white portion over the knuckle. Scoring is based on the number of clean punches delivered with the white part of the glove. The ultimate prize is an Olympic gold medal.

Professional boxers wear no headgear, and bouts are scored by "decision," made by a referee and/or three judges who sit ringside. The winner gets a boxer's "purse" – money that is shared with their trainer and manager, and traditionally collected as cash directly after the fight. Arguably, the biggest purse for a single bout was received by US heavyweight Mike Tyson, who was paid over $30 million for his 1997 fight against Evander Holyfield.

Dispelling a few misconceptions

Boxing was a widely popular spectator sport until the 1970s to 1980s – a time many consider to be its glory days, and which produced such charismatic champions as Muhammed Ali, Joe Frazier and Sugar Ray Leonard. For a while afterwards, though, it seemed to slump into the doldrums, struggling to regain a previously loyal fan base and polish up what had become a tarnished reputation.

Today things are very different: boxing is back, and positively basking in public approval. So what has changed? The answer lies with a number of welcome developments that have taken place in the sport over the last decade.

> *Boxing's safety record is greatly improved.* As a result, many other sporting activities (including gymnastics, horse-riding, hockey and even rollerblading!) are now judged to be more risky.

> *Women's boxing will be a fully ratified Olympic event in 2012.* It's official – it's OK for women to box. In 2009, female professional boxer Angel McKenzie made history when her bout at Bethnal Green's York Hall became the first ever women's boxing match to be televised live in the United Kingdom.

Angel McKenzie, female professional boxer

> *Boxing has returned to TV.* Millions now enjoy the entertainment offered by top-class fighters toughing it out in the ring, in a safe and controlled environment.

> *The sport has been reinstated as a strong part of our popular culture*, in film, TV and virtual gaming. Boxing is the most active game on the Wii Sports disk (this can be a good add-on to your boxing fitness training – but make sure you keep the wrist-strap tight, or your flatscreen could get knocked out!).

> *New national heroes are emerging from the sport of boxing all the time.* Examples include England's David Haye, who in 2009 became WBA Heavyweight Champion of the World; Ukraine's Klitschko brothers, both world heavyweight champions simultaneously; and "the darling of the Philippines," Manny Pacquiao, who holds nine world titles in seven different weight divisions.

>> Out of boxing – comes boxing fitness!

Hand in hand with these positive developments in the sport has come a much wider public recognition of the benefits of boxing training. Physical benefits, certainly: as discussed in the introduction to this book, competitive boxers are very fit athletes, with great stamina, strength, speed and co-ordination. Their heart and lungs are super-efficient; their body fat optimal; their muscular endurance second to none. If we train in a similar fashion, it follows that we can improve those things, too.

Perhaps even more significantly, though, people have now caught on to the psychological advantages of boxing training – advantages that are especially relevant to us today. The stresses that we may encounter in our daily lives aren't always simple, or easy to deal with. Faced with, say, a saber-toothed tiger, our prehistoric ancestors had the choice of fighting it or running away really fast: the "fight or flight" mechanism. But how do we escape from money worries, office politics, bullying at school or gridlock on the roads? The insidious nature of modern-day stress has been shown to cause disease, aggravate illness and impair judgment, concentration and self-control.

THE SCIENCE OF STRESS

When we encounter a situation that makes us feel stressed, it stimulates the fight or flight mechanism. This involves the release of chemicals such as adrenaline, noradrenaline and cortisol that help us deal with the perceived threat. As part of this process our airways widen, our breathing-rate increases, the liver releases glycogen (our main energy source) and fat into the bloodstream, our blood vessels and capillaries widen to get more oxygen to the muscles, our heart rate and blood pressure increase ... even our senses are heightened.

If we really were facing a sabre-toothed tiger, this reaction could save our lives. However, modern life often means that we feel this primal response in situations where we cannot channel it – for instance, at work or in a traffic jam. Then the chemicals accumulate in the body, and we soon feel the long-term effects of this build-up of stress.

So it's really important for us to find an appropriate outlet for our frustrations ... and what could be better than hitting the heavy bag, or putting together powerful punches in different combinations on the focus pads, all to the satisfying "thwack" of solid glove-to-leather contact? Boxing fitness provides a safe, non-combative environment in which to channel any frustration or aggression you may be feeling at the end of a difficult day.

And of course it's not just about the punching: some of the more technical elements in a boxing fitness program, such as skipping or speed-ball work, require discipline and concentration – helping to take your mind off anything that may be worrying you.

"

My job can be very demanding, so to boost my energy levels (and keep my sanity!) I've always tried to stay fit. Last year, though, I started to lose motivation – until I picked up a leaflet about boxing fitness classes in my local park. I did a few group sessions before progressing to private sessions with the trainer, who specializes in focus pad work. Believe me, I whack those pads! I love the liberty of being able to express my frustrations, and I'm definitely much more able to absorb the stresses at work.

Philippa, 46
Teacher for children with special needs **"**

Nor has the therapeutic nature of boxing training escaped politicians, education experts and teachers; more and more schools now incorporate boxing into their schedules as a curricular or club activity – and the number of youngsters registering with amateur boxing clubs is increasing all the time. More information on boxing fitness and young people can be found in Part Four of this book.

>> Who can benefit from boxing fitness?

We hope it's clear that boxing fitness can be enjoyed by almost anyone – and that different people will feel the benefits for different reasons. Because the training routine is so flexible, it can be adapted to accommodate most potential barriers to participation: for example, in Part Four we discuss some sensible precautions that should be taken by children under the age of 16 (who should not do heavy resistance work) and by older or less able-bodied people (for whom some of the more impactful elements of the training may be inadvisable).

But most of these precautions are basic common sense, and are applicable to any kind of physical exercise. If you're not sure whether you are fit to embark upon a new boxing fitness program, book a check-up with your doctor, tell them what's involved, and take their professional advice.

The fact is that boxing is no longer a working man's sport – and, reflecting this sea-change, boxing training has opened its doors to a much wider world. You can stay with the non-contact side of boxing fitness, enjoying a lasting relationship with a workout that never gets stale and always challenges you; or if you think you may like to take things further, into the realms of competition, you have the option of training for your amateur or professional boxer's license (see the Appendix on page 161 for information).

Finally, if you're tempted by competitive boxing but have passed the license age-limit of 34 years, you might like to consider "white collar boxing" – a fully regulated form of the sport that is open to men and women aged 25 to 57, and allows you to get into the ring in a competitive environment with added safety measures.

FIGHTING TALK

In the 1990s, a new phenomenon grew up in America after the famous New York boxing gym, Gleason's, staged a fight between two Wall Street businessmen with no prior fighting background.

These City types had bet on which one of them would remain standing after three rounds in the ring, employing trainers and working out for six months before the showdown at Gleason's in front of a huge crowd of colleagues and friends. Thus "white collar boxing" was born, and has become widely popular. If you want, check out the website www.wwcba.org to find venues and organizations that offer this kind of authentic boxing experience.

PART TWO >> THE PREPARATION

Having read Part One and learned about the many different ways in which boxing fitness can benefit you – whether you're a man or a woman, older or younger, just starting out or already quite fit – hopefully you're now ready to start as soon as possible!

This section covers everything you need to know in order to organize your training efficiently, and prepare for it properly. It's our experience that if your workout program suits your individual situation and lifestyle, you are much more likely to keep it up. Then, as you start to see visible progression, success breeds success – and you are well on your way to achieving great boxing fitness.

② Organizing your training

>> Establish your personal fitness goals

When starting out, it's important to be realistic about your goals and aspirations. What do you want to achieve from your boxing training? It's tempting to answer, "I just want to be fitter" – but what do you actually mean by that?

The word *fitness* tends to be used as an umbrella term, encompassing all of the different (usually physical) qualities that we can improve and enhance through exercise. Under that umbrella can be listed the following:

> Stamina, or "cardiovascular" fitness: refers to the efficient working of your heart, lungs and circulatory system

> Muscular endurance: the ability of a muscle or muscle group to repeat and sustain a particular movement, or series of movements

> Muscular strength: how much force your muscles can exert in a single effort – usually against some kind of resistance such as lifting a weight

> Speed: obviously, how fast you can perform a movement or series of movements

> Power: comprising both muscular strength and speed together

> Agility, balance and co-ordination

> Flexibility: often referred to as range of motion, or ROM

In addition, we could list *body composition*, which refers to how much of the body is made up of fat, and how much is made up of "lean tissue" (muscle, bone, tendons and ligaments). It is quite difficult to measure body composition: methods include underwater weighing, which is hardly practical, requiring a swimming pool and specialist equipment; skinfold calipers, accurate only when used by a skilled trainer (and rather unpleasant, since no one really likes having their fat pulled and pinched!); and calculations such as the body mass index (BMI), which tend to be far too broad-based and simplistic.

INSIDER INFO

Boxing fitness is a great way of losing weight – of reducing your *body fat percentage* relative to your *lean tissue mass*. It is generally considered ideal for a man to have around 10–20 percent body fat, and a woman, 15–25 percent – although this is influenced by many things, including personal preferences and cultural traditions.

If you would like to assess your body composition, your best bet is probably one of the many types of "body-fat scales" available on the market. These are like ordinary bathroom scales, but use mild electrical currents to determine total weight, body fat amount and percentage, muscle mass, hydration levels, and even bone mass.

Don't take the results as gospel, because they can be influenced by factors like how much you have eaten and drank, and the temperature of your skin; but if you follow the instructions carefully, you will get a reasonable idea of where you stand. Tanita is a manufacturer with a good reputation, but you can search the Internet to find scales that meet your requirements and your budget.

So keeping all the components of physical fitness in mind, try to be specific about your objectives. If your aim is to lose weight, that's great – boxing fitness can really help you shed the pounds. But how much do you want to lose, and over what period? Being realistic about this, and keeping track of your weight (perhaps by jotting it down in a training diary at the start of each week – see page 104), can help you achieve measurable progression and therefore maintain your motivation for exercise.

"

It feels like I have tried and failed at every single kind of diet. I buy the recipe book, the ingredients and the cooking equipment, and within a couple of days I can't be bothered and am right back to square one. So at the moment I'm cautiously optimistic, because I've found a personal trainer who is getting my weight down via a combination of boxing workouts and sensible nutrition. No fad diets – just careful eating and lots of cardio-based exercise. She makes me keep a food diary, which sounds intimidating but actually makes me much more aware of what I eat during the course of a day.

Jane, 50
Personal assistant

Cross training

If you're a runner or other type of athlete, you can use boxing fitness as a way to enhance your stamina, speed, recovery and so on. It's a good idea to set yourself targets, and to keep a record of any improvements in your sporting performance as you go along.

Here is just one example:

> A sprinter who can perform six 100-metre repetitions in an average time of 12.5 seconds might replace their usual hill-running interval session (which is undertaken once a week) with a boxing training session, over the course of a one-month period. All other sessions remain the same.

> The target is to improve their average sprint time – perhaps just to reduce it, or to bring it down by a given amount – by the end of that month. It is important to keep a note of the average time now, for the purposes of comparison in a month's time.

DECIDED ON YOUR GOALS?

As we've already mentioned, one of the beauties of boxing fitness is that it's a **total body workout**. It can also be tailored to address specific elements of physical fitness as listed in this chapter. At the same time it brings less tangible benefits, such as emotional health and well-being. But for most people starting out, we have found that *stamina*, *weight loss* and *general toning* are the most common concerns, so the first basic training session we describe on page 108 of Part Five is designed around these goals.

We then go on to show you how to vary the emphasis of your training if you want to tailor it to different objectives, or if you are ready to move on to an intermediate or advanced stage.

> At the end of the month, the sprinter would time themselves once again over six 100-metre sprints. If their average time was less than 12.5 seconds, this would represent evidence of relevant fitness gains achieved from the boxing training.

> It may be that they now take less time to recover between repetitions; that their speed has increased; and that their muscles are stronger. The combined result is improved sport-specific performance.

>> Planning your sessions

Once you've established what you're working to achieve, you need to plan your boxing fitness sessions so that they fit into your lifestyle as smoothly as possible. We're all pretty busy these days, and it can be hard to find room in our lives for ourselves – so when we do make the time to train, it's important that our efforts really get results.

When should I train?

This really depends on your personal situation and preferences. If you have a full-time job, you've probably got the choice of getting up early, exercising in your lunch hour, or training after work. Alternatively you can work out on the weekend – but because we're going to recommend that you exercise at least twice a week, and ideally three times (see page 16), that last option is not ideal. To recover properly, and so get the most out of your boxing fitness sessions, you should leave at least 48 hours between each workout – which means that realistically, you can only train once in any given weekend.

You may already know at what time of day it best suits you to exercise. Some of us are naturally morning people and can fit in a session before the day gets going, while others definitely aren't. You may need to find this out by a process of trial and error. But whether you are fitting your training around work, school, college or family life, try to find a regular window of opportunity where you can focus as fully as possible on you and your exercise session. This is *your* time. Rushing into boxing fitness without being properly prepared can lead to poor technique, compromise your results and even invite injury – so be aware, and be organized.

Your choice of when to train may also be affected by your eating and drinking habits. Again, this is a matter of lifestyle and personal preferences. We have found that some people can only work out if they have eaten shortly beforehand, while others really don't like to exercise too soon after food. There are no hard-and-fast rules about eating prior to exercise, but in Part Four we talk about the importance of good nutrition, and of "refueling" adequately after your training sessions.

How often should I train, and for how long?

If you want to see measurable results from your program, you should aim to work out at least three times per week. This may seem like a lot – but the good news is that a basic boxing fitness session can be done within just one hour, from warm-up to cool-down. On page 108 we show you how to structure your workout so that it fits into this exact timeframe, making it possible for you to include it relatively easily in your busy schedule.

Of course, training once or twice a week is still good, but it's only going to keep you maintained, rather than really kick-starting your desired fitness gains. And honestly, it has to be worth three hours of your time each week to feel more energized and confident; to be able to get into your favorite clothes again; and to hear people say: "You look great. What are you doing differently these days?" (If you get asked that question, say that you've taken up boxing training – and enjoy the reaction!)

As you progress through your program, you may find that your sessions are taking slightly longer than an hour. Physical training is a process of "overload and adaptation": our bodies become habituated to the work we are asking them to do, so that next time, they can carry out the same task(s) more efficiently. In effect, then, as the work becomes easier, our fitness gains plateau – and we need to challenge our bodies anew to get the same results.

In boxing fitness, one of the ways in which you can continue to challenge your body is by progressively adding more *rounds* (three-minute efforts) into a session. So, for example, you may advance from two to three rounds of shadow boxing, skipping and punching bag work, as a result of which your workout will be nine minutes longer – plus the extra minute of rest you'll need to take between each effort.

Don't worry, though: if time really is an issue for you, you can vary the intensity of your training in other ways (such as punching faster and/or harder, or incorporating some resistance work such as squats into your routine). This is covered in detail in Part Five.

Where can I train?

Another good question: here are your options.

1 *At a registered boxing club or gym*

Reflecting the sport's newfound popularity, ever-increasing numbers of boxing clubs and gyms are opening or expanding their activities. Many of them offer some kind of membership to the general public, alongside a range of boxing-related instruction and facilities.

To find a club near you, you can simply do an Internet search (for example, Google "boxing gyms + [your location]"); alternatively, you could contact the relevant national or regional division of the IBA –

International Boxing Association (www.aiba.org) – which is the amateur sport's international governing body – and they may be able to point you in the right direction.

If you go down the boxing club route, you might find that some of the websites look a little rough, with pictures of sweaty fighters baring their gumshields – and the gyms themselves can be rather scruffy if you're used to a health or fitness club. But don't be intimidated! Boxing clubs are usually very friendly, welcoming places; fees tend to be much lower than fitness-gym memberships; and the clubs are frequented by people from all walks of life, often forming a kind of community enterprise that runs social as well as sporting activities. They can really make you feel that you belong – and in addition you have all the necessary equipment and expertise on hand to get the most out of your boxing fitness program.

❷ *At selected health clubs and fitness gyms*

Many health and fitness chains conduct combat-type exercise classes for their members, in recognition of the dynamic, fun and therapeutic nature of boxercise (for the difference between this and boxing fitness, see pages 1–2). Increasingly, though, some of the larger chains are also introducing authentic boxing equipment into their facilities.

As well as making boxing equipment available to members, clubs are tending to employ either certified boxing trainers, or personal trainers with boxing qualifications; these professionals work one-on-one with clients to develop individualized training plans based around traditional boxing techniques.

All this is good news for you, if you live close enough to a suitably equipped health club or fitness gym. You can either take your boxing fitness program along with you and use the facilities, or, if funds allow, employ an on-site trainer to supervise your training and to work with you on the focus pads. Focus pad training is a lot of fun; it's covered in detail on pages 75–76.

❸ *In the garden, the local park – or even indoors*

If you live too far from a boxing gym or health club, or if resources are tight in terms of travel time or finances, don't let this stop you from boxing your way to fitness. On pages 125–27 we take you through a session that you can do pretty much anywhere, because it does not require much space. Provided that you have a few feet of clear space around you (to avoid damaging yourself, passers-by, or your fixtures and fittings), you can still enjoy boxing fitness.

And you don't need much equipment, either. Some of the techniques involved in boxing fitness can be practiced with only a small initial outlay on hand-wraps, a skipping rope and a stopwatch or other suitable timing device (go to pages 21–23 for more information about equipment). We list recommended products, vendors and online stores in the Resources section at the back of this book on pages 165–66.

INSIDER INFO

"Accountability," or having someone to answer to, is recognized as a key factor in training success: knowing that someone is waiting eagerly to exercise with you should get you out of bed on a cold winter morning ... or if it doesn't, ask them to come and dig you out. Regardless of how little you feel like exercising, and how tempting it might be to bail on it "just this once," make yourself complete your scheduled boxing fitness session. Inevitably, you'll be glad you did it, and be much more ready to face whatever the day has to throw at you.

Who should I train with?

Some people prefer to exercise alone, while others find that misery really does love company! If it helps motivate you to have someone else around to share your pain – or better still, to keep your mind off it – boxing fitness offers several options.

As discussed above, you can join a boxing gym or health club, where like-minded people may be happy to work out with you in a pair or small group. Boxing circuits, shadow boxing and punching bag work all lend themselves well to a class environment: simply enquire whether such sessions are being offered at your local facility. Sometimes they're even included in the general membership fees.

Alternatively, train with your partner, or take a friend or colleague along to the gym with you – making sure first that their fitness level and physical abilities are more or less comparable to your own; you don't want to hold each other back, or push each other too hard either.

What about a personal trainer?

More and more people are finding that they need a coach or personal trainer to get the best out of them when they're working out. This is partly about value for money: if you've paid up front for one-on-one training, you're less likely to cancel a session, and more likely to work your hardest during it. But it's also about having someone "in your corner." A qualified, empathetic fitness professional will design your program around *you*. They will listen to your concerns and your aspirations, and support, motivate and encourage you as you work toward your fitness goals.

So how do you go about finding a personal trainer who can help you specifically with your boxing fitness? As the benefits of boxing training become widely known, many personal trainers are now

Focus-pad training with a qualified instructor

making sure that they have relevant qualifications. If you'd like to go down this road, try to track down someone who is either a licensed focus pad trainer or an experienced boxing tutor. You could check out Google, look for printed ads in your local area or ask at your local gym. Alternatively, try contacting the various international and national associations of personal trainers for relevant information; you will find some helpful websites in the Resources section on pages 165–66.

If after all this you're still having trouble finding a suitable personal trainer, contact the publisher (see the copyright page at the front of the book for their address). They will forward your query to us and we will do our best to help.

Training by yourself

Finally, you always have the option of training by yourself. Lonely as this may sound, boxing fitness is actually really good for going solo – partly because it is quite rigidly structured in three-minute rounds, with one minute's recovery between each effort. By timing yourself over a specific interval, you can remain focused while devising personal challenges to ensure that you are constantly working to the max. (One example is to see how many skips you can complete in the space of a round; we provide plenty more advice on varying your training in Parts Five and Six.)

If you do train alone, remember that it's a good idea to practice some of your techniques in front of a mirror. In this way you can keep an eye on your posture and technique, and use your own mirror-image as a kind of imaginary moving opponent when practicing your shadow boxing and punching combinations.

ON TO THE PREPARATION

We've talked in some detail about establishing your fitness goals, and about where, when, how often and for how long to train. In fact, it will probably take you less time to decide such matters than it does to read this whole chapter. Do a little research; check in with work, friends and family if you need to, so that they're aware of your new regimen and will respect it; and you're almost ready to start.

First, however, we need to guide you through some important principles and practices to ensure that you are fully prepared and equipped for your new boxing fitness program.

③ Preparing for your training

>> What should I wear to my boxing fitness session?

Simple: all you need when starting out is loose, comfortable sports gear and a decent pair of running shoes. Depending on the weather, you can work out in shorts and a t-shirt or tank top, or in a tracksuit. Even if it's a warm day, it's a good idea to wear a number of thin layers that you can gradually shed as you progress through your session, and afterwards, put back on when you are cooling down.

As with any other type of exercise, avoid jeans, belts, buckles, intrusive zippers or studs, work shoes or boots, and bare feet. Take off any jewelery, tie up long hair, make sure your laces are secure, and don't chew gum. Sorry, but we still find on occasion that these basic things need to be said.

Although you can work out in a pair of ordinary running shoes, there is an argument for investing in a good pair of boxing boots when you get a little further down the line with your training. Some of the techniques you will be practicing involve agile footwork, with quite a lot of lateral movement in the lower limb. Running shoes tend not to support this area effectively, whereas boxing boots lace higher up the shin – sometimes even to knee level – to provide stability and protection. They are "breathable," allowing for the air to circulate and preventing sweat build-up; and they have rubber grip soles, giving you firm traction as you "bob and weave" like a champ.

Boxing boots don't have to cost the earth; you can get a reasonable pair for around half the price of a pair of specialist running shoes. For recommended products, vendors and online stores, see the Resources section on pages 165–66.

>> What should I bring with me?

In addition to wearing suitable training clothes, make sure that you have the following six items at hand for each and every boxing fitness session:

1 A towel. If you don't like to sweat, then boxing training is not for you! You'll need a small towel for wiping the sweat from your face, to make sure it doesn't get in your eyes, and for wiping your hands in case they become slippery – when you're skipping, for example. In any case, it is good gym etiquette to wipe down any shared equipment you may have been using during your session. Not only is this courteous to other members, it's also good hygiene practice.

2 A water bottle. Again, you will sweat a lot during your boxing session. It is very important that you remain adequately hydrated before, during and after your session; this is covered in more depth on page 86. Take plenty of water to your workout, and sip little and often throughout the session – this is far more effective at hydrating you than taking one long drink. Make sure that your water container is something that you can easily pick up and drink from, as hand-wraps and boxing gloves can turn the simplest actions into a challenge.

If you haven't eaten for more than a couple of hours prior to training, or if your session is likely to last much longer than an hour, it's a good idea to substitute water with an energy drink. Such "isotonic" or "sports" drinks replace fluid and electrolytes (essential minerals) that are lost through sweating, and contain carbohydrates to give your body an energy boost.

3 **A spare t-shirt or sweatshirt.** When you finish training, you will quickly feel cold in workout gear that is soaked with sweat. Make sure you have something dry that you can put on soon after your session.

4 **A way of timing your training.** Timing is an essential element in the boxing fitness regime. See page 29 for more information.

5 **A skipping rope.** Far from being a girl's game, skipping forms an integral part of any boxer's training regimen, building stamina and improving agility, balance and co-ordination (see also page 66). You will need a skipping rope for your boxing fitness program, and there is a huge range available – most costing very little. We recommend a lightweight plastic *speed rope*; again, check the Resources section for where to purchase one of these, but in fact most sports shops or department stores will stock them.

In terms of ideal length, you can check this by standing on the middle of the rope: the handles should reach just up to your underarm. But some people prefer their ropes shorter, and some longer, so you will need to experiment for

It's generally assumed that boxers wear hand-wraps – sometimes called "bandages" – under their gloves to protect their knuckles. In fact, the small, fragile bones in the wrists and hands are more vulnerable and prone to injury. Every professional boxing trainer has a unique way of wrapping their fighters' hands, and at elite level this is considered almost an art form – sometimes taking as long as 40 minutes to complete in the dressing room before a competitive bout.

Why should I wrap my hands?

Whenever you wear your boxing gloves (for punching bag or focus pad work) you must ensure that your hands are correctly wrapped underneath. There are three reasons for this:

> It helps you make a correct fist inside your glove.

> It prevents your knuckles from chafing against the leather.

> It also helps avoid potentially serious injuries.

It is quite easy to make slightly awkward contact with a punching bag or focus pad as you are learning, so take extra care to always use wraps. The small bones in your hands and wrists are delicate; they can take a long time to heal once damaged, so you need to take every precaution to protect them.

If you are borrowing boxing gloves from a gym, health club or fitness instructor, it is good hygiene practice to wear your own clean wraps underneath. The best boxing gloves are made of leather (see page 29) and cannot be washed – only aired. People will have worn the gloves before you, and others will wear them after. It makes sense on all counts to put on a pair of clean hand-wraps before you work out, and to wash your hands when your session has finished.

yourself. When buying, err on the side of too long rather than too short – you can always tie a knot in the rope under the handle if it's over-lengthy (this is also a good idea if buying a rope for a child who is still growing).

6 **Finally, hand-wraps.** No boxing fitness session is complete without these. In the following section we explain what they are, why you need them, which kind is preferable, and of course how to wrap your hands.

>> First things first: wrapping your hands

In addition to wearing suitable training clothes, at the start of your boxing fitness session – ideally, even before you warm up – you need to *wrap your hands*. Here we describe the traditional wrapping technique, but increasingly, gel- or foam-lined fingerless gloves are available as an alternative, to wear beneath your boxing gloves.

Although you will find hand-wraps provided at most clubs and gyms where boxing training is taught, we strongly advise you to buy your own for reasons of hygiene and comfort. They're not expensive (see the Resources on page 165 for vendors), and they're easily washable – though the color can tend to run, so if you're machine-washing them, don't put them in with your whites!

Even if you don't want to make heavy bag or focus pad work a major part of your boxing fitness workout, wrapping your hands is a good idea. For shadow boxing and speed ball work (see the techniques in Part Three), this has both a psychological and a physical benefit. As well as making you feel more professional and focused, wrapping your hands helps you keep them in the correct position as you make a fist.

Type and size of hand-wraps

Most hand-wraps are made of cotton. Some (often termed *Mexican* hand-wraps) incorporate an elastic-type material which make the wraps stretchier; this is the type we would recommend, as it gives a more snug fit and is slightly kinder on the skin.

Wraps vary as to color (up to you), width and length. We recommend a wrap that is no narrower than 2 inches. As for length:

> If you have small hands, a wrap of around 120 inches is ideal

> For medium to large hands you will need a wrap of 170 inches

If your wrap is too long you will know about it, because it will take you forever to bandage up your hands and you will end up with a big bunch of material in your palm – making it awkward and uncomfortable to close your hand into a fist. Too short, and you risk chafing or injury, as the wrap offers inadequate protection.

It looks complicated, how do I do it?

Wrapping your hands does take practice. Like tying shoelaces, it seems very difficult at first, but soon becomes second nature. If you have a trainer or a training partner, start by getting them to do it for you while watching and observing. Some people find that they can wrap one of their own hands easily, but the second one is more difficult – just keep on trying until you get the hang of it, or ask someone for help.

There are various ways of wrapping your hands: we'll describe the simplest and quickest way, and one that is very safe and effective.

1 Start with your hand-wrap rolled up. They come like this when new, but if your wraps are unrolled, then start again but rolling from the velcro-ed end and finishing with the thumb-loop at the outside of the roll.

INSIDER INFO

Hand-wraps do have a top and bottom – some are even marked "this side down" because you want the velcro to be face-up when you've finished wrapping your hands. If you find you started with the wrong side down, don't start all over again; on the last turn around the wrist, flip (or twist) the hand-wrap over and you will be able to fasten the velcro with no problems.

Cat has wrapped her own hands before helping Harry with his gloves

2 With the hand to be wrapped held flat, palm down and with fingers relaxed, put the thumb-loop around your thumb.

3 Wrap the fabric around your wrist 3-4 times, to ensure that it is well protected. Make sure that the wrap is firm, secure and smooth around your wrist but *not too tight* – you don't want to inhibit your circulation. To check, slip the ends of your fingers (of the hand doing the wrapping) underneath the edges.

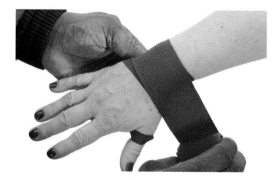

4 Moving back toward the hand, wrap across the top of your hand and around your knuckles 2-3 times. Keep your fingers slightly spread. The hand-wrap should form a cushion over your knuckles and extend just slightly over the ends of your fingers as they join your hand. Close and open your fist a couple of times, and wiggle your fingers: it's important that you can still do this comfortably.

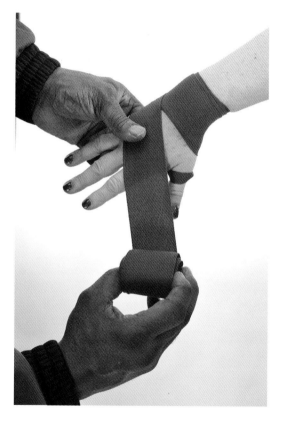

5 Bring the hand-wrap back around your wrist, and wrap around the wrist at least one full time. Then bring the wrap under your wrist and over the base of your thumb. Wind the fabric around your thumb and back over the top of your hand. You are aiming to cover all the areas of skin that are visible – you are literally wrapping your hand like a parcel, so that none of it is exposed.

6 Pass the wrap around the knuckles once more, then do figure eights – crossing over the back of your hand, around your wrist, back over your hand, around your knuckles. The illustrations make this process clear.

7 As you start to run out of material, make sure that you finish at the wrist. Wrap around the wrist one final time and secure the hand-wrap with the velcro strip.

8 Repeat all of the above with the other hand. Great! You are now ready to start your warm-up (go to page 35 for this).

CHECKLIST FOR SAFE AND EFFECTIVE HAND-WRAPPING

Do:

- Spread your fingers while wrapping, to ensure that the hand-wrap is not too tight
- Start and finish wrapping at the wrist – good wrist support is essential to avoid injury
- Make sure that the whole hand is covered, the thumb securely wrapped, and a cushion of material lies over the knuckles
- Check that during the process, and at the end, you can still wiggle your fingers and make a fist comfortably; the wrap should not feel awkward, bulky or constrictive
- Re-roll the wraps after you've finished, making sure they are dry before you do so (you can leave them on a radiator for a while)

Don't:

- Leave the wraps off because you think the gloves offer enough protection: they don't
- Give up! Keep practicing – it will become easier each time you do it
- Use wraps that are still wet with sweat from your last session; this can cause blisters
- Start your session with wraps that feel too tight or are otherwise uncomfortable – undo them and start again until you are happy

>> Other equipment

Top row from left: bag gloves, sparring gloves, boxing boots, sparring gloves; bottom row: hand wraps, focus pads, skipping rope

So far in this chapter, we have discussed the minimum personal equipment you will need in order to box your way to fitness. It's great that you need so little to start – but there are also many ways of enhancing the basic workout, if you are fortunate enough to train where any or all of the following items are available.

The boxing clock – and the importance of rounds

FIGHTING TALK

As we have mentioned, competitive boxing matches are measured in "rounds": regular intervals of fighting, followed by regular intervals of rest. Because of this, boxers structure their training around the same intervals of time and therefore need a way of measuring rounds during their workout.

In professional boxing, rounds last for three minutes, while in amateur boxing a round is only two minutes long. Rest periods in both sports last one minute, during which time the boxers go to their respective "corners" of the ring for water, advice, support and treatment. The cry of "Seconds Out!" that you hear before each round is not a time-limit, but a warning to the boxer's corner-assistant – his "second" – to leave the ring before the fight resumes.

To indicate the passage of rounds, an essential piece of equipment in any boxing gym is the *boxing clock*. Traditionally, this is a wall-mounted electronic clock equipped with a single hand. The clock face shows 0, 1, 2 and 3 at each of the usual "quarter-hour" positions.

Each quarter-hour section on the clock represents one minute – so that the single hand takes three minutes to move from the zero to the 3. When it reaches the 3, a bell or electronic signal sounds to denote the end of the round. The hand moves on to the zero during the minute's rest, at which point

another signal tells the boxer to recommence training.

Traditional boxing clocks are a specialist item; they're expensive and require wiring, so unless you are training at a boxing club it's unlikely that you will encounter one – or want to invest in one. But there are affordable variations on the boxing clock available today, such as Title Boxing's *Personal Interval Timer*, which costs less than a decent stopwatch (see the Resources section on page 165 and look online for vendors). It can be a good idea to purchase one of these; alternatively, if you are training at home or in a gym which has a normal wall clock with a second hand, you can keep an eye on your rounds using that.

The last resort is your own watch or a stopwatch – but these really aren't ideal, because checking them will interfere with the flow of your workout (and is hard to do when you're wearing hand-wraps and boxing gloves!)

Boxing gloves

You will need boxing gloves if you are going to include punching bag or focus-pad work in your

Harry is wearing 8 oz sparring gloves

FIGHTING TALK

Sparring gloves come in different weights rather than conventional sizes – usually between 16 and 20 oz, although this can vary. Professional competition or "contest" gloves are usually 8 or 10 oz.

use sparring gloves. However, you may choose to do so (or be advised to by your coach or trainer) when starting out. Until you have practiced your punching techniques and are familiar with them, wearing light bag gloves could lead to injury if you make awkward contact with the heavy bag or focus pad. A sore thumb, hand or wrist can interfere not only with your training but also with your daily activities, so it's best to start cautiously.

Whichever type of glove you decide to wear for your training, the higher the quality you can afford, the better. Leather gloves are preferable to synthetic ones, because they last longer, softening and moulding to your hands over time – and they don't absorb the sweat.

Having said that, it's inevitable that any gloves lent by a boxing gym or health club will become smelly after a while, because they've been used by other members and can only be aired, not washed. So make sure your own hand-wraps are clean and fresh to wear underneath, or, if the hygiene thing bothers you, buy your own gloves. You can get a decent pair of leather bag gloves inexpensively: check out the Resources section on page 165 for vendors and online stores.

The punching bag

Working the punching bag enables boxers to practice their full repertoire of shots and combinations without hitting another person. The bag provides cushioned resistance and is used to build strength and stamina, enhance footwork, and improve defensive or evasive techniques. These training elements are covered in more detail in Part Three.

program. These techniques are covered in detail in Part Three.

For training (rather than competition), boxers use two types of glove, known respectively as *sparring gloves* and *bag gloves*. The former are used in the ring when two fighters are sparring – meaning that they are practicing contact boxing, wearing headgear and other protection. Bag gloves are used for any other punching work that does not involve contact with another boxer.

There are a number of differences between the two types of boxing glove, the main ones being that sparring gloves are more substantial and padded; they extend further up the arm, fastening firmly around the wrist area with laces or velcro; and the thumb is stitched to the body of the glove rather than being loose and moving freely, as with bag gloves. All of these differences are for both boxers' protection, and make sparring gloves heavier to wear than bag gloves and more expensive.

You will not be making contact with another person in your boxing fitness program, so you don't need to

The uppercut bag is on the left, the heavy bag on the right

There are a number of different punching bags available, each fulfilling a slightly different function. The traditional "heavy bag" that we usually associate with boxing is a large, sturdy cylinder, made of leather or a synthetic material and filled with some kind of padding. It is often, but not always, suspended on chains from the ceiling, and is designed to withstand repeated and powerful punches without swaying too much. Smaller versions move more when you hit them – requiring you to be more mobile in response.

Uppercut or "angle-cut" bags are shaped to facilitate angled punches, and speed balls are small, air-filled bags anchored at the top to a "rebound platform" mounted parallel to the ground; these improve speed and hand–eye coordination. Other punching bags include freestanding and floor-to-ceiling types. It is not within the scope of this book to describe each kind of punching bag and its use in detail, but there are good summaries, with prices and recommendations, to be found at www.fit-box.com or www.punchbag.org.

If you can get access to a punching bag at the gym, this type of training can form an integral part of your boxing fitness program. Even though you don't get hit back when you "work the bag," done properly it can be tough: think of Rocky, using frozen carcases hanging in the abattoir to toughen up his hands and prepare for his bout! Of course, we don't recommend such extremes – but punching bag work can be a satisfying, effective and therapeutic way to work out.

Buying your own bag for home use is always an option. If you choose the type that suspends from the ceiling, make sure that your ceiling can take the weight! It's advisable to get the bag mounted by someone qualified to judge this, and if possible to screw the fittings into a joist or other suitable strong fixture. Not only is the bag heavy, but it will swing around if you punch it hard, placing extra stress on the bolts and chains. Keep in mind too, when purchasing your punching bag, that some come as a package, inclusive of everything necessary to fit them, and some don't – so you may need to buy the brackets, hooks, and so on separately.

Working on the speed ball

If you decide on an alternative type of punching bag, we would recommend a freestanding type that is not too fixed or rigid when you punch it. Although such stability allows you to punch powerfully, there is little or no reciprocal movement in the bag. This means that you don't have to move in response, so you are sacrificing the part of your workout that improves your reaction time, balance, lateral head movement and footwork.

The boxing ring

The ring is another authentic piece of boxing equipment – and one you are highly unlikely to have at home! (If you do, we're jealous.)

The modern boxing ring is set on a raised, square platform of between 16 and 25 square feet, which is covered with padding and a durable canvas. There is a post at each corner of the ring; to these are fixed four parallel rows of ropes that form a flexible, continuous barrier against which a boxer can lean

A freestanding punching bag suitable for gym and home use

when fighting or sparring (hence the saying, "on the ropes"). These ropes are further secured by way of vertical strips, to hold them together and thus reduce the risk of anyone falling through them to the floor below.

Even though some health clubs are incorporating rings into their facilities for boxing and other combat-type activities, chances are you will only encounter one in a boxing gym. If you get the chance to shadow box or do some focus pad training in the ring, you should go for it. There is something about climbing through the ropes and standing up there on the canvas that really gets your pulse going – it's hard to define, but it's a rush that doesn't seem to fade, however many times you do it.

Focus pads

Focus pads are flat, hand-held mitts of varying size and design. There are some shown in the photograph on page 28 and you'll see them throughout the book.

Focus pads are made of dense foam or other filling, covered in leather or a synthetic material. One side of the pads incorporates a kind of pocket or "glove" compartment, into which the trainer inserts his or her hands before fastening a wrist strap or similar to ensure that the pads do not slip or fall off. The pads are then held by the trainer at different ranges and levels, and in different positions, for you to punch.

Focus pad work is possibly the most exciting, varied and rewarding form of boxing training, as well as being one of the most effective ways of getting you fit – fast. We cover the technique in detail in Part Three, and really recommend that you incorporate it in your program if possible.

The thing to emphasize here, though, is that focus pads are an instructor's tool, and it is important for safety reasons that only qualified trainers employ them as part of any boxing-type training. If you try to hold the pads for a friend or partner, and don't know how to position or move them properly, there is every chance that you might get hit by mistake, or suffer strain or injury in your hands or wrists.

Weights, cardio and other conditioning equipment

There is a range of other equipment that can be used as part of your boxing fitness training – to vary your program, and to enhance any or all of the individual fitness elements we list on page 13–14. In this we could include cardio machines, such as steppers, cross-trainers, treadmills or exercise bikes; weights (either free weights such as dumbbells, or fixed-resistance gym machines); and other conditioning equipment such as Swiss balls and medicine balls.

To a large extent the particulars of your boxing fitness workout will depend on what facilities are available to you. But in Part Six – which deals with training around your boxing – we address the importance of including some core conditioning work in each of your sessions, and recommend some appropriate exercises and equipment for strengthening the abdominal and other core muscles. We also suggest some ways in which weight (resistance) training and cardiovascular work – especially running, which every boxer includes in his or her regimen – can complement your boxing fitness training, making your sessions even more effective and further boosting your fitness gains.

4 The warm-up

You're ready and eager to start your new boxing fitness program. It's Session One, but don't rush into it. You should never, ever start any boxing fitness session "cold." By this, we don't mean simply that you should feel warm in terms of body heat (although this is important); we mean that every part of your body – your heart and lungs, your muscles and joints and, perhaps less obviously, your mind – should be in a state of full readiness for the particular type of physical exercise to follow.

Boxing training is vigorous and dynamic. If you neglect your warm-up, your training session will be less effective, your fitness gains compromised, and the risk of injury – either during your session or afterwards – increased.

THE COOL-DOWN

After training you should also cool down by performing some stretches while gradually allowing your body to return to its pre-exercise state. The stretches described below can also be used after your workout for this purpose. This is almost as important as the warm-up to prevent injuries.

>> Start with a pulse-raiser

Start each of your boxing fitness sessions with a "pulse-raiser" – a few minutes of light aerobic exercise designed to raise your heart rate, lubricate your joints and increase the elasticity of your muscles.

The pulse-raiser can be something as simple as jogging slowly around the park or gym, or even on the spot if you don't have much clear space to exercise in. Alternatively you could ride to your session on your bike, or use one of the cardio machines at the gym (step, cross-trainer, bike) when you get there. Even brisk walking will do. Whatever pulse-raising activity you select, keep your limbs nice and relaxed, and your breathing under control throughout.

>> Progress to stretching

After around five minutes, when you are a little out of breath and your skin is feeling flushed, it's time to stop and stretch. Here are a few stretches that we practice with clients before each boxing fitness session, to ensure that they are properly limbered up and ready to start their session.

Static versus dynamic stretching

Most of us are familiar with static stretching, which involves performing a safe and correct stretching technique to the point at which you feel a gentle tension in the target muscle or muscle group(s). You then hold this position for 10–15 seconds before relaxing out of the stretch.

Athletes have traditionally undertaken static stretching both before and after a workout or competition, to help prevent injury, reduce muscle soreness, improve flexibility and enhance athletic performance. However, some recent studies have advocated the use of what is known as dynamic stretching prior to exercise, as being more effective in achieving these goals.

Dynamic stretching may be defined as "using sports-specific movements to prepare your body for the particular type of activity to follow." If you choose to focus on dynamic stretches before your boxing fitness session, static stretches then become the focus of your post-workout routine, when your muscles are warm and elastic – helping to increase the range of motion at your joints and generally aid recovery.

We have found that a combination of both types of stretching works well for a warm-up, and suggest below a number of exercises which will prepare you for your boxing training. Always ensure that you do a pulse-raising activity beforehand, and feel free to devise your own brief stretching routine. Vary this if you get bored; there are plenty of good sites on the Internet that cover a whole range of safe and effective stretches. Whichever you choose, prior to each training session ensure that you do at least one stretch for each of the following parts of your body:

> the neck

> the shoulders

> the chest

> the back (upper and lower)

> the waist

> the thighs (front and back)

> the calves

> the ankles

As we've already emphasized, boxing is a full body workout: don't just focus on your arms because you think it's all about punching.

MAINTAIN GOOD POSTURE THROUGHOUT YOUR STRETCHES

At all times during your stretching (and ideally, throughout your session) think about your *posture*. Good posture will help you avoid strain or injury during training – and the more you work on it, the more it will transfer into your daily life, helping you carry yourself taller, straighter and with more confidence. Here are a few pointers:

1. The ideal standing posture is with feet hip-width apart and facing forward.
2. Your knees should be "loosely straight"; in other words, your legs are not locked but nor are they very bent.
3. Keep the natural curvature of your spine, so that your lower back is neither hollow nor rounded.
4. Your shoulders should be held gently down – you can think about this in terms of having a "long neck" – and your chest lifted with eyes looking straight ahead.

>> Static stretches

❶ Neck

From standing

- Let your head drop gently down to your chest and hold this position for 10–15 seconds, feeling a good stretch down the back of your neck.
- Then raise your head, and turn it to look over your left shoulder; be careful not to let your right shoulder lift up – keep the neck long.
- After 10–15 seconds, take your head back to the central position and repeat over your right shoulder.

❷ Shoulders

From standing

- Raise your arms above your head as if you are stretching your hands up to the ceiling.
- Push them up as far as they can go without your heels lifting from the floor.
- Hold this position for 10–15 seconds, relax, and repeat a few more times.
- This is a really nice stretch to greet the day with!

❸ Shoulders/upper back

From standing

- Cross one arm over the front of your body at shoulder level, holding it above the elbow with your opposite hand.
- Pull gently with the "holding" hand until you feel a good stretch in the opposite shoulder and upper back.
- If you need to intensify the stretch, you can rotate your torso in the direction of the stretch – but make sure your hips remain facing forward.
- Maintain the stretch for 10–15 seconds, before relaxing and repeating on the other side.

❹ Chest

From standing

- Link your hands behind your back.
- Straighten your arms until you feel a stretch across the front of your chest.
- To intensify the stretch, attempt to raise your hands toward the ceiling behind your back, ensuring that your arms remain extended.
- Be careful not to round your upper back when you do this exercise: keep your head and chest lifted.
- Hold the stretch for 10–15 seconds, relax, and repeat.

❺ Waist

From standing

- Raise your arms above your head.
- Beginning with a bend over to one side, continue this movement (under control!) around to the front (you are bent at the waist, your upper body parallel to the floor) and back up the other side – so that effectively, you are drawing a large imaginary semi-circle with your upper body.

If you have any problems with your lower back, start this exercise very gently and only make small circles with your body until you have warmed into the stretch.

- Repeat five to six times, before switching to the other direction.

⑥ Lower back/back of thighs

From standing

- Cross one leg over the other.
- Keeping your legs loosely straight, drop your upper body down *gently* towards the floor until you feel a good stretch down the back of your back leg.
- Hold this position – don't bounce – while at the same time focusing on rounding your lower back (think of this as trying to push the middle of your back toward the ceiling). After 10–15 seconds, relax, stand up, and repeat for the other leg.

⑦ Front of thighs

From standing

- With your weight on your left leg, bend the foot of your right leg up toward your buttocks, grabbing hold of that foot just below the ankle with your right hand.
- Try to keep your knees together – and your balance!
- Then pull gently on the raised foot, in toward your buttocks, to achieve a stretch down the front of your right thigh.
- If you need to intensify this, you can open up the angle at your right knee by pulling the foot slightly upwards and backwards.
- Hold for 10–15 seconds and repeat on the other side.
- For fun, once you have achieved a balanced position, try to close your eyes and see how you wobble – making sure you have something to grab hold of if necessary, so you don't fall over!

8. Calves

From standing

- Position yourself a few feet from a wall and, leaning forward, place both hands against the wall at chest height.
- Take a step forward with one leg, keeping both heels on the floor but bending your front leg at the knee; your back leg remains straight.
- Then lean into the wall so that you feel a stretch up the back of your back leg, in the calf area.
- Hold for 10–15 seconds, relax, and repeat.
- To stretch your lower calf, closer to your heel, bend your back knee slightly too – still keeping the heel on the floor. You should feel the stretch move downward.

9. Ankles

Seated

- Sit towards the edge of a chair, hands on either side of your buttocks as illustrated.
- One foot remains flat on the floor; the heel of the other foot is in contact with the floor with the toes pulled upwards towards your knees.
- Slowly rotate your foot to draw imaginary circles in the air. Do a few rotations in one direction, then change direction for a few more.
- Repeat on the other side.

>> Three dynamic stretches

Stretch 1

From standing

- With feet hip-width apart, keeping your head and chest lifted, squat down as if you were about to sit on a chair but then stopped halfway.
- Your heels should remain on the floor and your feet and knees face forward throughout.
- As you squat, swing your arms down by your sides and a little behind you.
- Then stand back up from the squat, bringing your arms forward and up into a stretch above your head.
- Perform this exercise 12–15 times in a fluid motion.

Stretch 2

From standing

- Begin with bent arms, hands up by your shoulders in a "don't shoot!" position.
- Then reach forward with your hands until they are stretched out with your arms parallel to the floor at shoulder level.
- At the same time as you push out with your hands, round your upper back and tuck your head down between your shoulders.
- Return to the start position, retracting your arms and bringing your head and chest back up.
- Repeat 12–15 times.

Stretch 3

From standing

- With your legs wide apart, bend at the waist, dropping your head and torso down gently as you let your arms dangle toward the floor.
- Reach diagonally with your left hand to touch your right foot, and then the other way, so your right hand touches your left foot.
- Alternate this movement quite rapidly and fluidly so that in effect, your arms are swinging back and forth and your upper body pivoting slightly with each change.

If you have any problems with your lower back, replace this exercise with the following:

- Stand with your hands on your hips and, keeping your hips facing forward at all times, rotate your torso to one side (as if trying to look behind you).
- When you feel the natural limit of the stretch, twist back to your center, and turn to the other side.
- Repeat this cycle 8–10 times.

>> Moving on

Having read this section of the book, you now know how to organize yourself and prepare thoroughly for your boxing fitness program. You have the right clothing, equipment and personal supplies at your disposal; you know how to wrap your hands; and you understand the importance of a full warm-up and stretch. You're officially ready to begin to box. Here goes!

PART THREE >> THE TECHNIQUES

This section of the book covers the real nitty-gritty of boxing fitness. Here we show you – literally blow by blow – how to carry out each of the techniques safely and effectively, to ensure that you are getting the best possible results from all your hard work.

Some of the training elements take time to master, and can be quite frustrating when you are starting out. One example is skipping: if you've never "jumped rope" before (or if the last time you did it was a long, long time ago), it can make you feel clumsy and self-conscious. Don't let it; we urge you to persevere. Even trying to complete a round of skipping will bring you fitness gains, however many times you have to stop and start again. And it's worth all the effort when you finally get through a full three-minute interval without stumbling and swearing.

Before you make a start on this section, and learn how to stand and punch, make sure you have read Part Two thoroughly so that you are fully prepared and warmed up for your training session.

5 Stance, punches and combinations

>> The stance

One of the first and most important techniques you need to learn is how to stand, which is also known as your *stance*.

Why is a good stance so important?

A good stance allows you to punch with power and speed while staying grounded and stable. It also enables you to move around nimbly on your feet in different directions without losing your balance. This is known as *footwork* and is covered in more detail on pages 56–60.

If you work from an incorrect stance, bad habits may form which eventually could lead to strain and even injury. Having said that, don't worry too much at first! It takes time to get it right. Just bear in mind the following guidelines each time you train.

If you are right-handed, you will generally use what is called the **orthodox stance**, with your left foot forward and your right foot behind.

Both boxers are in an orthodox stance

Left-handed boxers are known as **southpaws** – the word is thought to come from baseball. If you're a southpaw you stand with your right foot forward rather than your left.

INSIDER INFO

Practice taking up your stance in front of a mirror whenever possible: it's the best way of seeing what mistakes, if any, you are making. When done regularly it can stop you from feeling self-conscious when training at the gym.

For boxing fitness, it doesn't actually matter whether you prefer an orthodox or a southpaw stance – there are no rules to dictate one or the other. If you're not sure, simply do it by instinct! Stand up, raise your hands like a boxer, don't think too much, and step forward. Whichever foot you put in front, this is probably your most natural and comfortable stance.

For ease of reference, all the descriptions that follow are for the orthodox stance. Southpaws should follow the instructions but use the opposite arm and foot to lead. We have included footwork and upper-body illustrations to help you.

1. From standing, take a step forward with your left foot. The lateral distance between your feet should be about 18 inches; any less, and you'll be "walking a tightrope" which will adversely affect your balance.

2. Your front foot remains facing forward. Angle your back foot outward (clockwise) to approximately 45 degrees (or ten past the hour).

3. Bend your knees slightly. If you bend your knees too much you will be squatting, which will strain and tire your muscles. This position should be comfortable.

4. Your weight should be distributed evenly between both feet. Shift your weight onto the balls of your feet, ensuring that your knees remain comfortably bent. In this position you should feel solid and grounded.

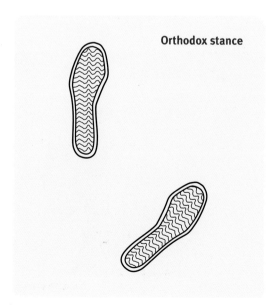

Orthodox stance

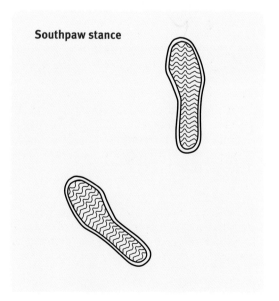

Southpaw stance

5 At this point it's likely that your whole body is facing forward. Instead, position yourself slightly sideways-on to your imaginary opponent. Your front foot, hip and shoulders should be in line, with your left shoulder and hand a little in front of the right.

Orthodox guard

What do I do with my arms?

1 Make like a boxer! The classic "hands up" position is known as the *guard*: to achieve it, raise both hands, each making a loose fist as illustrated. Your elbows should be bent and tucked into your chest.

2 Your left hand is held slightly out in front of your face, with your elbow slightly extended toward your imaginary opponent and ready to throw a punch. The fist is at the level of the top of your shoulder, palm facing inward toward your body.

3 Your right hand is held further back, fist close to your chin: think that you are protecting your chin, ready to block a punch. The palm faces inward, as with the left hand. Your elbow stays close to your ribs.

Great! Follow the above guidelines and you will have achieved a good stance. Almost every technique you learn in this book will be performed from this stance – it's your *home position*, so it pays to practice and get it right.

Southpaw guard

CHECKLIST FOR A CORRECT STANCE

Do:

- Make sure your chin is down but your eyes are looking up
- Keep your shoulders naturally rolled forward
- Relax your neck and shoulders
- Ensure that you're comfortable: if you feel off-balance, stand up straight, shake it out, and try again

Don't:

- Worry too much at first: stance is a personal thing, so work at it until you find what is right for you
- Switch feet. If your stance is orthodox, your left foot should always stay in front – and vice versa
- Feel any tension in your arms, shoulders or neck

either begin or end with the jab, this is the punch you should practice first.

If you have chosen to stand in an orthodox position with your left foot forward (see page 46) you will always jab with your left hand – the lead hand. Southpaws, your lead hand, the one you jab with, will be your right hand. Here's how to do it:

1 In your stance, with both hands making a loose fist, throw out your lead (left) hand until your arm is fully extended. The movement comes straight out from the shoulder, and the hand remains at shoulder level.

2 Keep your right hand up, close to your chin, with your chin tucked down.

3 As your left arm extends, rotate it so that at the end of the movement, your hand is facing palm-downward.

>> The punches

There are four main punches used in boxing: the **jab**, the **cross**, the **hook** and the **uppercut**. Each of these can be delivered singly or in various *combinations*.

When you begin your boxing fitness program, you will practice the punches in isolation; the respective techniques are carefully described and illustrated here. But as you become more familiar with the shots, and your fitness levels improve, you will start putting your punches together, making your workout more challenging – and more fun!

The jab

You're probably familiar already with *the jab* – the most important punch in any boxer's repertoire. Jabs can be used both defensively, to keep an opponent at bay or out of range, and as a highly effective attacking shot. Since most boxing combinations

The jab

4 At the imaginary point of impact, the *knuckled* part of your hand (meaning the knuckles and the lowest joint of your four fingers) makes contact with your imaginary opponent. To avoid any injury to your hand, it's important to keep your wrist strong so that it doesn't bend. Your thumb remains naturally curled in, touching the second joint of your index finger.

5 Immediately after your arm has reached its full extension, reverse the jab movement, returning your hand to its original position.

> If your preferred stance is southpaw, perform the movement exactly as above – except that you will jab with your *right* hand.

As you progress in your boxing fitness program, and depending on your personal fitness goals, you may use the jab to develop speed and power, to practice defense, or to make contact with the punch bag or focus pads at different levels and in different positions. For now, though, focus on technique and build your jab into a strong, confident shot.

The cross

After the jab, you need to learn *the cross*. If you work from an orthodox stance, you will throw the cross with your back hand – your right – delivering it to your imaginary opponent across your body (hence the name). The right cross is also known as the "straight right." Of course if you're a southpaw, you'll deliver the cross with your left hand.

FIGHTING TALK

"It's a knockout!" The cross is a powerful punch and, performed effectively, accounts for a large percentage of the knockouts in professional boxing. In the ring, boxers usually open up their opponent with the jab and follow it directly with the cross – delivering the classic one-two combination that we know and love.

1 Take up your stance. Ensure that your weight is over the balls of your feet, and both hands are up in the guard position, tucked closely into your chin. Remember: elbows in, chin down, eyes looking ahead.

2 Keeping your left hand close to your chin, throw out your right hand toward your imaginary opponent's head. You should be standing sideways-on (see page 47), so it should come naturally to deliver the shot across your body. *Don't* lift your right elbow laterally, toward the horizontal, or you will be straying into the realms of *the hook*.

3 As with the jab, during the punching movement you will rotate your arm so that at the moment of impact, when your arm is fully extended, the knuckles are uppermost and the palm facing down (while still keeping your hand in a loose fist).

The cross

4 When your arm has reached full extension, retract it by reversing the movement, bringing your hand back to the guard position.

So far, so good – but it's not a very strong movement. If you simply punch out using your arm alone, you achieve little real power or reach; you'll be doing a karate type of punch, not a boxing one. To get some oomph behind the cross, you need to use your upper body too.

5 Try the straight right again, this time driving off your back foot and pivoting your hips and shoulders into the punch. Keep balanced, and ensure that your back foot doesn't leave the ground. Your upper body thus moves square on to your opponent, but only for the time it takes to throw the shot; when you retract your hand back to the guard position, the hips and shoulders pivot back too, so that you are once again sideways-on – back in your boxer's stance.

Much better. With your bodyweight behind the cross, you can deliver a strong, straight and powerful shot – it's a great feeling. But don't be tempted to stand and admire your own work! Get back to your guarded stance as snappily as possible, ready to throw the next punch.

> Southpaws, reverse the instructions given above. Remember: you jab with the right hand, and cross with the left.

The hook

The next punch to learn is *the hook* – perhaps the most difficult shot to master, and one that requires lots of practice. Don't worry, though: by the end of this section we'll have you throwing hooks like a champ!

The hook is often described as a "semi-circular" punch, designed for delivery with the lead hand to the side of an opponent's head or chin.

Of necessity, we break down this rather complex punch into its component parts – but as you get better at it, you will be able to join each phase of the movement together to deliver a smooth shot.

It can help to understand the hooking movement if you think about how you would slam a door shut. Note that you will usually hook with your lead hand – left for orthodox, right for southpaw – but not always.

1 In your stance, with your hands up in the guard position, lift your left elbow toward the horizontal. In this way your elbow and fist are both at the same level as your shoulder, all parallel to the floor. At the same time, draw your elbow back slightly; this opens up the angle at your shoulder joint in anticipation of the hooking movement of the punch, and aids the momentum.

The hook with rear hand

When throwing a hook, it's important that you keep a tight angle at your elbow joint – about 90° or slightly more. If you increase the angle your hook will be long and looping, easily anticipated, and much less powerful. You could also connect awkwardly with the bag or focus pad, risking injury to your hand, wrist or shoulder.

2 As you draw your elbow back, ensure that you have a "horizontal" fist – your knuckles should be uppermost and pointing forward, with the palm of your hand down and your thumb tucked loosely against your index finger. Keep your rear (right) hand close into your jaw, to protect your chin.

3 To throw the punch, keeping your elbow fixed, you then need to pivot your hips and upper body sharply in a clockwise direction – which naturally propels the fist through a tight arc across the front of your body, into the point of contact (which, if you were in the ring, would be with the right side of your opponent's head or chin).

4 At the same time as you rotate your torso and hips, pivot your lead foot clockwise so that the left heel moves slightly outwards. Everything is now moving together to bring the hook to a powerful conclusion.

5 Upon contact, the hook's circular path ends abruptly: pull your hand quickly back into the guard position.

Once you've mastered the hook, you can throw it at different angles; for example, a boxer may target the lower body as well as the chin or head.

The uppercut

The uppercut is the fourth and final punch you need to learn before starting to put together your combinations. It is the only "vertical" shot in boxing. Rather than being delivered straight out from the guard like the jab and the cross, or around the side like the hook, it is thrown *up* toward the target – which is generally an opponent's chin, but can also be lower down, on their body.

An uppercut is usually, but not always, thrown with the rear hand – so that would be the right hand for orthodox and the left for southpaw.

When choosing to throw an uppercut, a boxer needs to be in fairly close range to their opponent – sometimes called "fighting inside" – so that they can get their bodyweight under the shot and deliver it with sufficient force.

To throw a right uppercut from an orthodox stance, here's what you do:

1 Start in your stance, with your back (right) knee slightly more bent than usual. By lowering your right shoulder, drop the same side of your body into a semi-squat position – remembering to keep your left hand up, close to your chin.

2 Now rotate your right hip and shoulder forward, at the same time pushing off the ball of your back foot and thrusting your right fist upward in a rising arc toward your imaginary target. Your rear heel will naturally raise a little and turn outward.

3 As you punch upward, it's important that you pivot your hand so that it is palm inward toward your body; the knuckled part – rather than the side of the hand, thumb-uppermost – must finish the shot. It's also important that you

Left-hand uppercut, southpaw stance

>> Punching combinations

The four punches you have learned can be thrown in isolation, or you can repeat them any number of times – for example, *the double jab*, when two jabs are thrown one after the other. They can also be mixed up in groups known as *combinations*.

Stringing your shots together is fun, and challenges you both mentally and physically. In the ring, the most eye-catching combinations are performed fluidly, at high speed and with technical expertise – and when you try it yourself, you'll see how tiring that can be. In fact, just try punching out in front of your body, or up into the air above your head: left-right-left-right in continuous succession, as hard and fast as you can. After just a few seconds you will feel your heart rate go up and your muscles start to fatigue.

There are a number of basic combinations you should begin with, and these are described in the pages that follow. When you've practiced these and feel confident with them, experiment with your own. The idea is to build up a varied repertoire, which, when performed over a three-minute period and incorporating *footwork*, is the basis of *shadow boxing* (see pages 56–60 and 64–65).

All the combinations described on page 54 onwards assume that you are starting in your stance – whether orthodox or southpaw – and with your guard up (see the pictures on page 47). It's important to master the individual shots before moving onto these combinations, or you really won't get as much out of the workout.

Remember to complete each punch correctly so that it sets you up for the following one. This includes your *recovery* from each punch. If you don't, your weight will not be in the best position to deliver the next in the sequence. Boxing combinations flow. They feel right when you deliver them correctly. You can't really practice one combination enough – repeat it, until it almost becomes second nature.

keep a tight, fixed angle at your right elbow. If you straighten your arm, the punch loses its power.

4 To complete the uppercut, retract your right hand quickly, back to its guard position close to the chin. Your hips and shoulder return in a clockwise direction to their starting position, as you take up your stance once again.

5 For a left or "front" hand uppercut, your left knee is bent and the left shoulder lowered. Then quickly transfer your bodyweight to the ball of your left foot, punching upward with your left arm – keeping it bent, at a right-angle – and pushing up with your knees at the same time. It's a short, sharp movement.

Your stance: a reminder

The chin is tucked down, but the eyes look up at all times.

The rear hand protects the chin, ready to block an opponent's punch.

The lead hand is held close to the chin and a little in front of the rear hand, ready for the jab.

The lead foot, hip and shoulders are in line, with the lead shoulder and hand a little in front.

The guard: the classic "hands up" position of the boxer.

The elbows are held in close to the body.

The body is held slightly sideways-on, to maximize the power and reach of the punches – and to protect the boxer from body shots.

The knees are slightly bent, ready for the delivery of a shot or for deft footwork.

The rear foot is angled outward slightly, to enable it to pivot for more power behind the punches.

In the orthodox stance, as illustrated, the left foot is forward and the right foot behind (southpaws will reverse this).

The feet should be at least 18 inches apart laterally for a good, grounded stance.

The weight is balanced on the balls of the feet.

PUNCHING COMBINATIONS: 1-10

Number	Name	Description	Comments
1	**Double jab**	Two jabs in quick succession	Throw out two jabs, one after the other.
			Don't rush or "paw" at your punches; at the end of the first jab, make sure you extend your arm to its full reach before bringing the hand back into the guard position. Then deliver the second.
			Make your punches sharp and snappy.
2	**One-two**	A jab, followed by a cross	Throw a jab. When your jabbing arm has reached its full extension, and your hand is coming back to your chin, begin to throw the cross from your rear hand.
			The second punch should follow smoothly from the first (one-two, not one ... two ...): let the momentum carry your arm through.
			As you deliver your cross, remember to emphasize the rotation of hips, torso and shoulders – to get power into the shot. When you've completed the punch, hips and torso pivot back to their starting position.
			Make sure after both shots that your hand comes back to the guard position by your chin, rather than dropping down below shoulder level (and leaving you open to a "counter" – an answering punch – from your imaginary opponent).
3	**Double-jab cross**	Two jabs in succession, followed by a cross	Just as it sounds: perform *Combination 1* and then follow through with a cross.

Number	Name	Description	Comments
4	**One-two-three**	A jab followed by a cross, finishing with another jab	Perform *Combination 2*; add a final jab. Focus on achieving a smooth transition from punch to punch. Shoulders, torso and hips should pivot fluidly and your bodyweight should be nicely balanced throughout.
5	**One-two-three-four** (also known as **four straight**)	Jab, cross, jab, cross	As for *Combination 4*, but finish with a cross. Again, make it fluid and balanced.
6	**One-two-hook**	Jab, cross, hook	As for *Combination 4*, but instead of being a jab, your third punch is now a hook (a left hook if you stand orthodox; a right hook if you're a southpaw).
7	**One-two-uppercut**	Jab, cross, uppercut	As for *Combination 4*, but instead of being a jab, your third punch is now a lead-hand uppercut.
8	**Jab-hook-cross**	As it sounds	Throw out your jab. Follow it with a hook (remember, this will be on the same side as your jab), and end the combination with a powerful cross.
9	**Jab-uppercut-cross**	As it sounds	As for *Combination 8*, but after your jab you throw a lead-hand uppercut before finishing with your cross.
10	**Jab-uppercut-hook-cross**	As it sounds	With the exception of the "four straight" (*combination 5*), this is the first combination to string four punches together instead of three – so it demands even greater balance and attention to technical detail.

6 Footwork

Because the simple act of punching draws on so many elements of fitness, you can achieve a lot in boxing training simply by throwing combinations. For example, if you spent one three-minute round with your feet remaining still but your arms repeating *Combination 5* (four straight) for the whole period, you would be working pretty hard. Throw the punches as fast and with as much power as possible, and you'd work even harder.

But you can drastically enhance the effectiveness of your boxing fitness session if you add *footwork* into the mix. There's a reason why Mohammed Ali's famous quote didn't just say "Sting like a bee"; it's equally important for a boxer to "Float like a butterfly." A fighter who is lumbering and flat-footed will be limited in the power they can generate in their punches. They will be easy prey for a deft opponent – who may literally run rings around them – and are unlikely to be able to maneuver into an advantageous position for landing their own shots.

So, when you are comfortable with your punches and combinations, start to think more about what you're doing with your feet.

>> Footwork when punching

As we have seen when discussing the individual punches, your feet play an important part in generating power in your shots, and establishing a fluid technique when delivering them. Here's a reminder of what your feet do in the four punches:

> **The jab**: your lead foot can remain stationary when you jab, or it can step forward – to bring you closer to your opponent, and help you punch with more power. You can also jab while retreating. Whether you actually move your feet or not, your bodyweight should be on the balls of your feet and shifted slightly over the front foot as you snap out the punch.

A right cross with plenty of power behind it

> **The uppercut**: for a lead-hand uppercut, the vertical thrust of the shot is greatly aided by a powerful upward drive from the front foot and bent front knee. When initiating the shot, your bodyweight is shifted over the ball of the lead foot. For a rear-hand uppercut it happens pretty much in reverse: your weight shifts slightly to the back foot, which, together with the back knee, pushes powerfully upwards to aid the vertical punch (the heel of your back foot pivots outward slightly during this movement, and returns to normal as you resume your balanced stance).

So, don't underestimate the role of your feet in boxing fitness training – even when you're standing still and punching.

INSIDER INFO

You will note that, with the exception of the jab, you don't actually move around when throwing individual shots and combinations. It's tempting to dart in and out like a pro while punching, but in fact you need to find a balanced, grounded position as you set yourself for your shots. Once you have mastered the punching techniques, it will become obvious that the important shifts in bodyweight discussed above can only be achieved from such a position – and this is doubly the case when stringing shots together in combination.

> **The cross**: little power is generated in the cross without the aid of the lower body. As you pivot your hips into the punch, you drive off your rear foot to achieve a strong momentum. The heel of that same foot may rotate outward, following the movement of the hips. This is fine – as long as the whole foot doesn't lift from the ground (it can help to think about an imaginary bolt going through the front of your foot, anchoring it to the floor). When you retract your hand to the guard position, your bodyweight shifts back, so that it is balanced once more over both feet in the stance.

> **The hook**: for this punch, most of the power derives from a strong rotation of the torso and hips, driving the lead arm and fist along their horizontal path into the target. As this occurs, your lead foot also pivots, with the heel moving outward slightly to contribute to the strength of the shot. Once again, when the punch has been delivered, the heel returns to its original position and bodyweight is balanced over the balls of both feet in the stance.

>> Moving between punches

Now you need to learn how to move *between* punches. This will enhance the cardiovascular part of your boxing fitness workout, as well as toning your muscles and improving your speed, balance, co-ordination and agility.

Once you hit the heavy bag you need to move those feet to get out of the way as it swings back at you!

The first thing to note about boxing footwork is that you remain, as far as is possible, in your stance. You may remember that standing square-on is not advisable for boxers, since it leaves them open to body shots from their opponent, and impairs their balance and their ability to deliver powerful punches. So how are you doing at this stage? Use the boxed text to recap on your technique.

If you have checked and are happy with your stance, you are ready to move like a boxer. The following instructions apply to the orthodox stance; southpaws, simply substitute right for left and vice versa.

Moving forwards and backwards

1 To advance, simply step forward a little with your left foot, pushing off your back leg as you do so. Don't lunge – it's more a shift, or a shuffle. Make sure that, as you step, your body retains its sideways-on alignment, and don't let your legs stiffen.

2 When you have stepped with your front foot, slide your right (back) foot forward. The aim is to return to your exact same stance as when you started, but just a few inches further forwards.

3 Throughout, check your guard. Are your hands up close to your chin, with your chin tucked down and your eyes looking up and ahead? Your elbows should remain tucked into your body, and your shoulders rounded forwards a little, so that you are in a semi-squat.

4 To move backwards, simply reverse the above. Shift your rear foot backward, and move your front leg back to regain the stance.

Moving laterally

This is a little more awkward to do while retaining your stance, as you'll see. The important thing to remember is to *move the foot closest to the desired direction first*.

1 To move to your right, push off your left (front) foot and step sideways slightly with your right (back) foot.

2 Then move your left foot in the same direction, the same distance, to shift your body over and regain your stance. You'll need to do this a little more quickly than when moving forwards and backwards, because when you step over to one side your hips open out a little and you are temporarily more square-on to your imaginary opponent.

3 To move back to your left, push with your right foot and step to the left, following with the right to bring your body back to the stance.

Whichever direction you are moving in, this "push stepping" or "rolling" kind of action won't feel natural until you've practiced it. When you get used to it, though, it becomes second nature and you can speed it up, moving in different directions fluidly and with ease.

The crouched position and movement involved in boxing footwork is great exercise for the lower body. It's especially rewarding for the ladies, toning and strengthening any areas of concern, such as the backside and inner thighs.

>> Developing your footwork

With the basics under your belt, you can experiment. Have fun and mix it up! Try moving and then punching – first individual shots, and then combinations. As long as you're in motion and challenging your heart, lungs and muscles, you are getting fitter. Here are a few suggestions for some footwork drills.

1 Take a step to the front and then throw a quick jab. Recover from the jab by sliding your rear foot forward far enough to return to your original stance.

2 Try the same with a double jab.

3 Try moving backward and then jabbing.

4 Move sideways, to the left or to the right; when you have stepped, throw a one-two, a one-two-three, or a four straight – and move back to your original position. Add in some other combinations, by referring to the list on pages 54–55, or devising your own.

And why not make it a little more complex still:

5 Move your right (back) foot clockwise slightly, and behind you. Almost simultaneously pivot the ball of your left foot, and your left hip, in the same direction to retrieve your balanced stance. Then throw some shots. If you continue to move like this, you will in effect circle your imaginary opponent. It is as if your left foot were the center-point of a clock, and your right foot moving around the outside of the clock face. A line drawn between your left and right foot would be the clock's hand.

6 On your toes, with your guard up, bounce forward and backward as if you were taunting an opponent by deftly moving in and out of range – though always remaining in your stance. Think to yourself: "in-and-out, in-and-out, in-and-out"; establish a rhythm.

7 Then try doing the same thing laterally ("left-and-right, left-and-right, left-and-right"). And you might add in some "bobbing and weaving," which is an evasive or "dodging" technique – covered on page 62 ("in-and-out, bob-and-weave, in-and-out, bob-and-weave").

In addition to practicing drills such as those recommended above, and your own that you will come up with, a great way to improve your footwork is by *skipping*. This is an integral part of any boxer's training regimen, and one you will master in the course of your boxing fitness program. You will – even though that may be hard to believe when you start out!

7 Defensive and evasive techniques

Nimble footwork is an essential part of a boxer's defense, but it is by no means the only one. It's alright to just move your whole body out of range to avoid being hit, but if you never stand your ground, you'll never land any scoring punches of your own.

So a fighter has to be able to dodge, block or ward off ("parry"), and respond to an opponent's punches while standing in front of them. The defensive and evasive moves with which they achieve this lend another dimension to boxing fitness training. Of course, since you're not getting hit, you don't need to parry. But dodging and countering are useful additions to your repertoire when shadow boxing, working on the punching bag, or doing focus pads.

>> Ducking, slipping, bobbing and weaving

If someone is aiming a punch at your head, it makes sense to move it. It also makes sense not to move it by rearing backward, exposing your chin! So as you practice your boxing fitness, bear both these things in mind and try the following evasive drills – always in your stance, with your guard up.

Ducking

Just like it sounds – simply bend your knees and with a straight back, duck down. Imagine what will happen to your opponent's punch: it will miss you entirely.

Training benefit: the ducking movement strengthens and tones your leg muscles, as well as sharpening your reaction times.

Ducking a punch while retaining your guard and stance

Slipping

To slip an imagined incoming punch, rotate your body slightly (by pivoting the hips and shoulders); the blow would pass harmlessly next to your head. You can also use slipping to block a shot to the body: if you are rotating your torso clockwise, tuck in your left elbow tightly to your body so that it would block the punch – and vice versa for an anticlockwise slip.

Slipping to the right to avoid a southpaw jab

Training benefit: the slipping movement works your oblique (side) and abdominal muscles – which is great for the waistline – as well as sharpening your reaction times.

Bobbing and weaving

This involves lateral, ducking and rolling movements. A punch is coming – bend your legs quickly and shift ("bob") your body to the left or right of the blow (think of it like a side bend).

To return to the upright, central position, make a rolling or weaving motion with your upper body, as if you were coming underneath the blow that has missed you. (If you stood straight up, you would effectively make your head a target again.) Throughout, keep your guard close to your chin, your chin tucked down, and your elbows close into your body.

Training benefit: the combined movements work your oblique (side) and abdominal muscles, strengthen and tone your leg muscles, and sharpen your reaction times.

Returning to the stance via a weaving motion beneath your opponent's punch

>> Counter-punching

Once you have practiced the individual evasive techniques and can perform them fluidly, both in isolation and in combination, try adding some punches into the mix. Duck, slip, or bob and weave around your imaginary opponent's shots, and then counter – answer back – with some of your own.

You can counterpunch with single shots, or with any or all of the combinations listed on page 54–55. Each time, ensure that you have recovered your balance from the evasive move and regained a good, grounded stance before you punch; and remember to check that your hands return to the guard position, remaining there until the next counter.

You're the boss, make up your personal repertoire! Throw a jab, roll underneath the imagined counter, then throw another. Double the initial jab, and then double the counter-jab. Or deliver a flurry of blows (one-two, one-two-hook and jab-uppercut-cross), ducking or bobbing and weaving between each combination. In terms of boxing fitness, it really doesn't matter what you choose to do. The point is that you are working hard physically in your movements, and engaged mentally in your techniques.

After the slip, countering with a straight right

8 Shadow boxing

Shadow boxing entails pitting yourself against an imaginary opponent, and moving around as if the two of you were actually fighting in the ring. When you shadow box, you basically combine all of the techniques we have covered so far in this section:

> punching + defensive/evasive moves + footwork

And you put it all together solo – almost literally "boxing at shadows."

Many people find this element of boxing fitness to be the hardest – not so much physically (although it can be very taxing), but more because it can make you feel self-conscious. Try to persevere, it does get easier.

As part of your boxing fitness program, shadow boxing will greatly enhance your general conditioning, as well as serving to fine-tune your technical skills. It will also contribute to that therapeutic, stress-busting training effect. Once you stop feeling silly – and you will, if you give it a proper try – you can achieve a calm focus which takes your mind off a hectic day, or personal problems that you're having difficulties channelling.

> **"**
>
> The first time I tried shadow boxing, I felt like an idiot. I kept expecting someone to shout, "The other guy has left the ring, mate!" But I persevered and now it's second nature. It prepares my muscles and my mind for the session. It gets me in the zone.
>
> David, 29
> Amateur boxer **"**

FIGHTING TALK

Boxers will always do a number of rounds of shadow boxing prior to both training and competition. It functions as a dynamic warm-up (see page 36). This helps them focus, as they try out various combinations and strategies for dealing with a sparring partner or opponent. It is a valuable conditioning tool.

Here is our advice, when starting out.

1 **Try it in private first.** Of course, you may be training on your own anyway, so the silly feeling won't be so much of an issue (a bit like singing to yourself in the shower – it's OK as long as no one else can hear you). But if you're doing your boxing fitness in a gym or health club with other people around, you will probably feel more comfortable practicing a bit on your own, beforehand.

2 **Just do it.** If you are training in public, don't think too much about what you look like or what other people may think. Try it, and have a laugh. Punch out, punch up, punch all around ... it doesn't matter; if you're doing it, then you're getting fitter. Make it fun, because your workout should be fun.

3 **If possible, shadow box in front of a mirror.** Use your own reflection as an "opponent"; that way, you can judge the angles and positioning of your shots while checking that your guard remains up, your chin is tucked down, and so on. (The slight downside of this is that your footwork will be a little more limited than if you were shadow boxing in the ring, or in an open space.)

4 **Time your rounds (see page 29).** From the outset, attempt to shadow box over a period of three minutes – a round. Of course, you may need to stop, catch your breath and "shake it out" several times within that time period, and that's fine. But piecing together a three-minute round gives you a defined target for starting and completing your efforts, and has the attendant psychological benefit of achievement when you are able to say, "I did this many rounds of shadow boxing today!" Make sure you take a full minute's rest at the end of each round. You can add rounds as you get fitter.

5 **Pace yourself.** As you'll find, three minutes can feel like a long, long time – so pace yourself. Set yourself small, measurable goals, such as running through each of the ten combinations given on pages 54–55, five or ten times, with a ten-second rest in between each set. This helps to focus your mind on something other than fatigue, and seems to make the time pass quicker.

Finally, don't give up. Sometimes shadow boxing can be frustrating. You don't feel balanced; your punches seem rusty; nothing is coming together right. This is normal and, as for all of the training elements in boxing fitness, with time and practice you will become more fluid and proficient. Check out the training programs in Part Five for advice as to how to incorporate shadow boxing into your sessions, and how to progress.

⑨ Skipping

Of all the training elements involved in boxing fitness, skipping is perhaps the hardest to describe with the written word. Essentially, if you haven't done it before, you simply have to grab a rope and try it!

Although skipping can be very frustrating until you master it, persevere. Don't give up. After all, nothing worthwhile ever came easily, and once you've become proficient with the basics (and you *will*), you can find lots of different ways of using your rope to get fit. This chapter is intended to start you on your way, but don't feel limited to the simple techniques we describe here. There are no rules: find your own system, and your own rhythm.

>> Why boxers skip

Hopefully, it is apparent by now that there's a good reason behind each and every element involved in traditional boxing training – and skipping is no exception. Rope work is great for building endurance: boxers will skip for varying numbers of rounds, challenging their heart, lungs and muscles by adding more three-minute efforts, or skipping faster and/or harder through them.

Skipping also plays an essential role in developing balance, co-ordination and agility. Boxing requires these skills both for the effective delivery of punches and combinations, and for dextrous footwork.

It can take competitive boxers months, even years, to perfect their advanced skipping techniques. Remember that, just like you, they all started from scratch and built up their skills with lots of practice.

>> Where to skip

For your health and safety it's important to find a suitable surface on which to skip. If you jump on a hard, unyielding surface you may experience stress injuries to your feet, ankles or knees, while on an irregular floor there are tripping hazards.

If possible choose a shock-absorbing jumping surface such as a wooden sprung floor or a gym mat (one that won't slip from under you). If you're training outside, you might find a running track or a tennis court with a forgiving surface. Skipping on grass or firm sand is unlikely to injure you as long as your ankles are strong and stable, but it may prove difficult to get into any kind of rhythm if your rope gets snagged.

Your rope may also get caught up in baggy pants or long laces, impeding your flow and frustrating you. So choose appropriate clothing. In terms of footwear, we advise wearing a comfortable, supportive pair of running shoes to skip in. You may have purchased boxing boots for your program; these are great for shadow boxing, punching bag and focus pad work, but won't provide sufficient cushioning for skipping, which is an impact activity.

When you're ready to start, check that there's no one and nothing in the vicinity that might get tagged by your rope!

>> How to start

Once you have selected a suitable rope of the right length for you (see pages 22–23), and a safe place to skip, you're ready to go. If you've never skipped before, this is how to begin:

1. Stand with a balanced posture holding one handle of the rope in each hand. The mid-section of the rope is resting on the floor behind your feet.

2. Swing the rope forwards over your head, using a small circular movement of your arms and hands – initiated from the elbow.

3. As the rope descends in front of you and reaches the floor, attempt a small double-footed jump over it, so it clears your feet. You don't need to jump as high as you might think!

4. If the rope clears your feet, try to keep its momentum going with a continued motion of

your arms, so that it carries on in its circle back over your head and down towards the floor.

5. Then jump again and keep going. You are now officially skipping.

6. If the rope doesn't clear your feet, return to the starting position and try again. And again...

Expect some initial frustration, and focus on the positive: last week, you only managed between three and ten rotations of the rope at any one time; today, you've skipped for 30 seconds without tripping. And build on your progress. The day you manage to skip through a full three-minute round without stopping is truly an occasion on which to congratulate yourself.

>> Advanced skipping

When you have mastered the basic two-footed technique, try some different skipping styles. Remember that even though you may be stop-starting your way through the rounds, you are still improving your fitness. You're in constant motion, your heart rate is raised, and you are working your lungs and muscles over a sustained period. The point isn't just being able to do it; it's about continuing to try.

Some different skipping techniques

> **Running in place.** This is a natural progression from the small double-footed jumps, but you may even find you prefer it from the outset. The technique is just as it sounds: remaining stationary (meaning you don't actually travel as you "run"), lift your knees high with each turn of the rope as if you were running in an exaggerated way. With each knee lift – left, right, left, right – the rope makes one full rotation.

> **Traveling with the rope.** You can do this with either technique – double-footed jumps or running (high, alternating knee-lifts as above). Simply move along the floor as you skip. Travel

forward, backward and from side to side. You can work the perimeter of an imaginary square, or make up your own shapes.

> **One-footed skipping.** Get into your rhythm with the double-footed jumps. When you're skipping fluidly, pick one knee up and hold it there, continuing to turn the rope so that you are effectively hopping on one leg. Perform several rotations on that side before swapping to the other. If you get to a confident place with this, try traveling (see above) while you hop!

> **Double-unders.** Now we're straying into impressive territory! If you really want to emulate a boxer, try making two turns of the rope for every one double-footed jump. You'll find that in order to succeed, you need to jump higher, and spin the rope much faster.

> **Cross-overs.** This technique is very advanced. As you skip, cross your arms at the elbows on the downward arc of the rope. Jump through the loop of the rope that forms in front of your body,

then uncross your arms on the next downward swing. Continue to criss-cross the rope in this alternating fashion. Good luck!

INSIDER INFO

Don't be too ambitious at first: try adding in just a few double-unders during the course of a round of basic skipping. You may need to stop and "regroup" after each one – it's surprising how much faster it can make your heart beat! Work on the transition between your double-unders and your basic skipping rhythm; in time you'll develop the ability to perform several consecutive double-unders – or even do a whole minute without stopping. (Double-unders on one leg, anyone?)

10 Punching bag work

There are many different kinds of punching bags available – see the equipment section on page 30 – each serving slightly different functions for the boxer in training. Generally, working on the punching bag:

> builds stamina and power

> improves punching speed, reaction time and reflexes

> fine-tunes technical skills – not only in the punches and combinations, but also in footwork and defensive/evasive moves

For your boxing fitness program, and depending on your access to facilities, the ideal punching bag to begin on is a fairly solid one. You want a bag which moves a little when you hit it, but which doesn't swing or spring about all over the place. The surface should provide a good resistance to your shots, with some give – but not allowing your glove to sink into it without a trace! If the bag is too soft it will be exhausting work trying to get any snap into your punches, and your technique will suffer. If on the other hand it is too unyielding, your hands and wrists may become sore from the impact.

>> Prepare properly

Before you do any punching bag work, you need to have wrapped your hands carefully (see page 23), and over your wraps you must wear boxing gloves. You can choose either sparring gloves or bag gloves (see page 29); remember that if you wear the heavier kind of sparring gloves this will add another dimension of effort to your workout.

Don't use the punching bag wearing only your wraps: we have come across people who do this to "toughen themselves up," but however authentic it may make you feel, you risk seriously damaging your hands.

Wear a pair of running shoes or boxing boots that grip well, especially as the floor where you are exercising might be slippery (or become so as the sweat begins to fall!) Ensure that you have your towel and water bottle close by – punching bag training is, and should be, hard work.

INSIDER INFO

If you find that your knuckles are getting a little sore and chafed from your boxing training, try cutting an ordinary bath sponge in half and placing one half on each hand, over the knuckles. Then wrap your hands as normal, over the top of the sponge.

>> How to hit the bag

In terms of fitness alone, it doesn't really matter how you hit the punching bag – just doing so repeatedly will work your lungs, heart and muscles. However, your workout can be more challenging and satisfying if you use the bag to practice a repertoire of shots

Take up your stance in front of the bag

and combinations, learning to improve technically as you go along.

1 To begin with, position yourself in your boxing stance within arm's reach of the bag. If you stand too close, you won't be able to deliver your punches with any range or power: in other words, you will cramp your own style. And if you stand too far away, either you will miss altogether, or you will be off-balance as you move and/or over-reach to make contact with the bag.

2 With your guard up, throw out a jab. Remember that the jab is a straight punch, extending out from the shoulder with the hand, elbow and shoulder in alignment. (If you need to, brush up on your punching technique with a few "shadow jabs" before tackling the bag.) Make sure that when your hand makes contact with the bag, your wrist stays strong and doesn't bend. Keep your other hand close to your chin in the guard position, and your chin tucked down.

3 Once you have completed the punch and your jabbing hand is returning to the guard position, the bag may sway back toward you – depending on how heavy it is. Move out of the way if necessary, in whatever way feels natural. Duck, slip, or bob and weave ... as you become used to a particular bag's responses to your punches, you will learn to maximize the training benefits of such evasive and defensive reactions (see pages 61–63).

4 Throw another jab, or a cross. Or a combination. Uppercuts are difficult to perform on a basic cylindrical bag, but you can angle the shot "to the body" rather than delivering it vertically "to the head" if a specialized bag is not available.

5 As you feel ready, remember what you've learned about footwork (see pages 56–60) and start to move around the bag – always with your hands up and in the correct stance. Circle around to the left, and to the right, getting used to the feeling. When you want to punch, stop

Throw a jab, keeping your wrist strong

moving and throw the shot(s), then move again. Mix up the footwork – for example, you can try bouncing on the balls of your feet, forward and backward, as if you were moving in and out of an opponent's range. The important thing is to keep in motion.

Build up your efforts with measurable progression

Even if you have a good base fitness level, you'll find this type of training tough going at first. Aim initially to work the bag over, say, 30-second intervals with a short break in between. Then gradually build up your efforts, with the ultimate objective of maintaining a good-paced workout over a full three-minute round.

This may take some weeks, so make sure you keep a record of your progression – it's very rewarding to see those effort-intervals increase. When you do get to the stage of working over complete rounds, be certain to take a full one-minute rest between each.

DIFFERENT FITNESS ELEMENTS

As you become proficient on the punch bag, you can alter the emphasis of your work to focus on speed, stamina, strength, power, agility, balance, co-ordination and so on. We include some specific recommendations for this in the training programs in Part Five, but the principles are quite simple:

- To build speed, throw your punches and combinations quickly, and make your footwork fast.
- To build stamina/muscular endurance, punch repeatedly over longer periods of time and/or with less rest.
- To build strength and power, hit the bag as hard and powerfully as you can.
- To build agility, balance and co-ordination, concentrate on deft footwork and evasive/defensive techniques in response to the bag's movements.

You can also vary your workout by throwing punches at different levels and angles. For example, imagine that your opponent is very tall. To reach their head with a jab, you need to aim your punch higher than your own shoulder-level: aim high on the punching bag. Imagine that they are shorter than you, but that you want to aim a shot to their body: bend your knees, "drop down" and throw a straight shot low on the punching bag. Use your imagination, and your punching bag session will never become stale.

>> The speed bag

Boxers use the speed bag to improve their reflexes and hand–eye co-ordination. We've included it here, rather than giving it a stand-alone chapter, because it is a specialized piece of gear and may well not be available at your local gym or health club. It's also really difficult to master, and won't give you the noticeable fitness gains of some of the other techniques. But if you get the chance to try it, here's a quick lesson in how to go about it.

1. When using the speed bag, you must wrap your hands; it's up to you whether you choose also to wear bag gloves. The equipment should be adjusted so that the bottom of the ball is level with the bottom of your chin. Stand square on to the speed ball, rather than in your stance, and hold both hands up in front of your face, loosely fisted.

2. Hit the ball gently with the side of one fist (the little-finger side), using a small forward movement. The bag will swing back, hit the board, come forward, hit the board, swing back, and hit the board. When the bag comes forward once more, try hitting it again with the same hand. It's very tricky to time this right at first. Keep trying.

3. It can help to think about drawing an imaginary circle that goes outward from your face, round, and back in toward your body. On the outward part of the circle, the side of your fist makes contact with the ball. Your hand continues the circle back in toward your body; at the same

time, the speed bag is responding to your punch by knocking against the board as described above. As your hand completes its circle and starts another, it makes contact with the ball again – and so on.

4 When you seem to be getting somewhere, and can hit the ball in a regular, repeated rhythm with one hand (1-1-1-1), try doing the same with the other hand (2-2-2-2). Then alternate two on each side (1-1, 2-2), or single punches with each hand (1-2-1-2). Mix it up. Make up your own combinations.

The most important thing with the speed bag is to be patient. When you first try, it's likely to go all over the place, but keep trying. It really is a matter of timing and co-ordination.

11 Focus pads

In the section on equipment (see page 33) we described what focus pads are, and stressed that they should be the tool of a *qualified trainer only*. Be very wary of trying the pads with a friend, or with someone you met at the gym – either or both of you could get injured.

Having said that, if it is at all possible, try to build focus pad work into your boxing fitness program. Of the many types of training that we do, with clients of all ages and abilities, it's most often the focus pads that get them coming back for more.

There are several reasons for this. Focus pads are:

1 *The closest you can get to real boxing, without hitting anyone or getting hit.* Although the punching bag (see pages 70–74) provides a target for you to hit, and resistance to your punches, it cannot provide the flexibility and variety of the pads.

2 *Really interactive.* The trainer takes the initiative, calling out punches, combinations and other moves; you respond and react

The trainer holds the focus pads in the correct position for a jab (gloves would be worn)

accordingly. Although many aspects of boxing fitness training can be done alone, it's great to share the experience sometimes, and to receive feedback and guidance.

3 *A type of training that ensures measured progression.* If you've found a good instructor and work out regularly with them on the pads, they will know your fitness and ability levels. They will therefore be best placed to tailor-make your individual sessions, and your broader program, to ensure that you achieve steady gains that are relevant to your goals.

4 *Flexible – so easily adjusted "on the spot."* You've had a good night's sleep, eaten well and feel fine; why won't your body respond during training? Alternatively, you've had a late night out and a few beers, and crawl to your session;

how come it's your best yet? Your focus pad coach will know this is just how it goes sometimes, and instinctively adjust the pad work to reflect your needs *on that day.* Essentially, your goal for each boxing fitness session is to feel "positively extended," not exhausted and demotivated. There's a fine line: a good trainer will draw the line in just the right place.

So try to find someone qualified to hold the focus pads for you on a regular basis. In-between times you can rehearse and reinforce what you have learned on the pads in your shadow boxing and punching bag work. In terms of the techniques involved, the same principles and practices that we have covered throughout Part Three apply. We include some advice on how to find a suitable focus pad instructor in the Resources section.

This section of the book is concerned with matters that may not be directly related to boxing fitness, but which are nonetheless essential to your ongoing health, safety and well-being during your exercise program. These matters include:

- **Nutrition and hydration**. Eating well, and drinking sufficiently of the right kind of fluids, will not only keep you healthy but also significantly increase your chances of achieving your fitness objectives.

- **Injury prevention and treatment**. If you follow the advice given throughout Parts Two and Three, you are unlikely to get injured as a result of your boxing fitness program. But there are some minor ailments that can occur, such as sore knuckles; dealing with these promptly and effectively is key to getting back on track and in full training as quickly as possible.

- **Health matters**. One of the great things about boxing fitness is that it is accessible to most people, regardless of age and ability. But it may be that you need to take certain precautions when embarking on a new and challenging training program – for example, if you are pregnant; a mature practitioner, and/or less able-bodied; or if you have a pre-existing condition such as asthma, heart disease or diabetes. This chapter offers some sensible advice to ensure that you work out at an appropriate level, remaining safe and well.

12 Nutrition and hydration

>> **The importance of a healthy diet**

We all know that a balanced diet is necessary for our health and well-being – and that this includes not only adequate food intake, but also sufficient fluid. Water is the medium by which all nutrients and chemicals travel and interact to keep us functioning at our best. It is therefore essential that in addition to eating enough of the right kinds of food, we remain optimally hydrated.

The human body needs food in order to rebuild or repair itself, and to provide fuel (energy) for its systems to function. There are three main groups of nutrients:

> Carbohydrate

> Protein

> Fat

Read on through the rest of this chapter for an introduction to these main food groups.

In addition, we require an intake of vitamins and minerals in order to help release the energy contained within the food we eat.

Starting on a new training program involves using more energy each day than your body is accustomed to. If one of your training goals is to reduce body fat (see page 14), that's great: weight loss will result when the energy you expend is more than the energy you take in. If your goal is not weight loss but, say, improved toning or stamina, then you'll need to eat more food to compensate for what you are burning off during exercise.

Whatever your individual fitness concerns and aspirations, to get the most out of boxing training your diet must comprise a healthy balance of all the nutrient groups. Here is a brief overview of each.

>> Carbohydrate

Functions of carbohydrate in the body

Carbohydrate fuels muscle contractions, and so is the main energy source for any exercise, including boxing fitness. It should make up around 60% of your overall dietary intake. Once eaten, carbohydrate is digested and used in the body in a number of ways:

> It is broken down into glucose – sugar – and carried in the bloodstream before being used by the tissues as fuel.

> Any carbohydrate that is not needed for immediate energy release is stored in the muscles and liver, as glycogen.

> Once the body's carbohydrate stores are full, any excess present in the blood is stored as fat.

The passage of glucose from the blood into the body's tissues is controlled by the hormone, insulin. Insulin plays a vital role in regulating blood sugar levels. If the body does not produce sufficient insulin, or its cells are unable to respond to the insulin that is produced, the disease known as diabetes results (see also pages 95–96).

Carbohydrate is the body's preferred source of fuel. In other words, you will burn carbs – as long as they are readily available – before you will burn protein and fat. If the body doesn't have enough carbohydrate to meet its energy demands, protein will be broken down to do the job. This can limit your ability to build and maintain tissues. Carbs are also an energy source for the brain and central nervous system, playing a vital role in activities which require thought, precision, dexterity and co-ordination. Activities such as boxing training!

Carbs are the main fuel for your boxing fitness session, so you need to make sure that you have sufficient stores available in your muscles to go the distance! How long your energy supply will last depends on the duration and intensity of your workout. As a general rule, if your session is much longer than an hour, or if you haven't eaten within two hours prior to exercising, you'll need to replenish your glycogen stores with a carb-rich snack or sports drink.

Types and sources of carbohydrate

Carbs may be simple (also referred to as "sugars") or complex (also referred to as "starches"). A third type of carbohydrate is known as fiber.

Simple carbs are easy to digest, and are thus readily made available to the body as fuel. Fruit is a good source, being cheap and convenient, as well as containing the micronutrients necessary to release the food's energy potential. Unfortunately, other (very tasty) sources of simple carbohydrates include cookies, muffins, candy and soft drinks such as cola; these contain excessive sugar and fat and should be limited in the diet, or ideally avoided altogether.

Complex carbs take longer to be broken down, absorbed into the bloodstream and stored or used by the body. This means that the fuel they contain is released more slowly over a sustained period, giving you a steady, constant energy supply.

doesn't provide the body with any energy, but may help lower blood cholesterol. It can also slow the delivery of glucose into the bloodstream, which in turn may reduce the risk of developing some forms of diabetes and coronary heart disease – as well as making you feel fuller for longer.

>> Protein

Functions of protein in the body

Protein has the following functions:

> It forms the framework of many bodily structures, including collagen (present in bone and connective tissue); keratin (present in the skin); and muscle tissue.

> Especially during endurance events or periods of fasting, protein provides a usable source of energy.

> It also regulates various bodily processes, such as controlling blood sugar levels and fighting infection.

Types and sources of protein

All proteins are made from amino acids, and there are twenty amino acids in total. Of these, nine are considered to be essential to the daily diet, because the body cannot produce them independently: in other words, we have to ingest them in our food.

Proteins containing all nine essential amino acids are known as *complete*. Most sources of complete proteins are animal-based (eggs, meat, poultry, dairy and fish). Plants such as grains, cereals, nuts, seeds and vegetables do contain protein, but they are *incomplete* sources, being deficient in one or more of the essential amino acids. So it is especially important, if you are a vegetarian, to include a variety of protein sources in your diet – thus making up your full complement of amino acids over the course of a day.

The nutritional value of complex carbs further depends on whether they are *refined* or *unrefined*. Refined carbohydrates (for example, white bread, pasta and rice) are generally processed, and so depleted of fiber, vitamins and minerals. Unrefined carbohydrates (for example, wholemeal or whole grain products; fresh and frozen vegetables) have not been processed to the same extent, and therefore are healthier choices.

Ideally, your diet will include plenty of complex, unrefined carbohydrates – to keep your energy stores topped-up, and to provide a steady, sustained release of energy. Good choices are wholegrain pasta and rice, sweet potato, porridge and breakfast cereals. Simple/unrefined carbs like muffins and cookies can give you an energy boost, but the "spikes" in blood sugar that they cause may leave you feeling low and tired at certain times of the day.

Fiber is basically indigestible plant material: it is found in fruits, vegetables, grains and beans. Fiber

Protein and exercise

Our bodies break down proteins continuously, recycling their component amino acids to build new proteins elsewhere. This process can be intensified during exercise, with the secretion of a hormone called *cortisol*. Cortisol acts to maintain the body's energy supply, by variously breaking down carbohydrate, protein and fats.

We have seen that the body's preferred source of energy is carbohydrate. When all the available carbohydrate has been used up, the body will then turn to protein as a source of fuel. So, depending on your diet, and on the duration and intensity of your boxing fitness session, some muscle tissue breakdown may occur as a result of your exercise program. It's therefore important to include some protein in all your meals, and to rest and eat well after each training session – thus helping to encourage and promote tissue growth and repair.

Protein should make up around 10% of your overall diet. If you eat too much, the excess will be excreted in your urine or used as fuel. If losing weight – reducing body fat – is a key fitness goal for you, keep in mind that just as your body will naturally choose to burn carbs before protein, so it will burn protein in preference to fat (see below). Thus, excess dietary protein can suppress the use of fat as fuel, potentially leading to an increase in body fat.

For this and other reasons, it's best to eat your protein as part of small, regular meals. Recommended daily allowances (RDAs) vary for each individual, and depend on many factors: Google your national Food Standards Agency and follow the links for more information.

> Your boxing fitness workout is energetic and endurance based, so may bring about muscle tissue breakdown. Make sure you include some protein in all your meals. Good sources are fresh, quality meat, eggs, raw nuts, whole milk, and canned beans or pulses in water. Your body can only use a certain amount of protein at any one time, so try to eat little and often. Processing and overheating your food will denature the protein in it.

>> Fat

Functions of fat in the body

Fats and oils – together known as *lipids* – have many important functions in the body, including:

> The formation of cell membranes.

> Assisting in the transmission of nerve impulses.

> Protecting the internal organs (although too much fat can inhibit their function).

> Transporting, storing and using some key vitamins.

> Insulating the body, thus helping to regulate body heat.

> Providing an energy reserve for the body.

Dietary fat is often vilified, being linked in the public consciousness with obesity, heart disease and other disabling conditions. But just like carbohydrate and protein, fat is an essential nutrient and should comprise around 30% of your overall food intake. Fat itself is not the problem – it is the type, source and amount that matter.

Fat has more than twice the calories per gram of both carbohydrate and protein, so diets high in any kind of fat are *energy dense* – in other words, they may lead to us taking in more energy than we use up, thereby promoting an increase in body fat. It is excessive body fat, not dietary fat itself, that is a danger to our health and has been linked to the development of disease.

Types and sources of fat

Saturated fats, which are solid at room temperature, are found naturally in meat, poultry, dairy and eggs, as well as in non-animal sources such as palm and coconut oils. Although studies have linked saturated fats with clogged arteries, in fact they are an essential part of our diet, enhancing the immune system and helping to promote healthy liver function.

Unsaturated oils, which are liquid at room temperature, fall into two main categories: mono-unsaturated and polyunsaturated. Sources of the first include olive oil, avocados, nuts and seeds; while the latter are found in oily fish, sunflower seeds and oil, walnuts, pumpkin seeds and sesame seeds.

Both types of unsaturated fat are necessary for health. Diets high in monounsaturated fats are thought to lower blood cholesterol levels, thus reducing the risk of coronary heart disease. Polyunsaturates are sources of omega 3 and 6 – substances which cannot be synthesized by the body, but are important for healthy cell functioning.

Even if losing weight (reducing your body fat) is one of your fitness goals, don't cut out fat from your diet. Just limit and balance your overall fat intake. Avoid skimmed or artificially low-fat foods: these have been processed and often padded out with trans fats. Instead, choose full-fat dairy, quality meats, seeds and oily fish, as well as butter, olive and coconut oil.

Trans fats, also referred to as **hydrogenated fats**, should be avoided in the diet where possible. Some do occur naturally, but the majority are a by-product of manufacturing, and are therefore present in heavily processed foods such as cookies, muffins, pies and pastries. Trans fats have no positive use in the body, but are simply stored as body fat – simultaneously preventing other, "good" types of fat from fulfilling their required functions.

>> A healthy diet

It is clear from the above that we need to consume a diet that is balanced in the three main nutrient groups, roughly in the following proportions (expressed as a percentage, by weight, of overall dietary intake):

> Carbohydrate: 60%

> Protein: 30%

> Fat: 10%

It is not just the balance of nutrients that matters: we should also be careful to select from varied, good-quality food sources. Many factors along the food chain – from soil to seed to animal welfare; from the use of chemicals for growth and ripening, to methods of transportation, manufacturing and processing – affect the quality of the food which leaves the farm and eventually arrives on our plates. It is important to make sensible, informed dietary choices that suit our lifestyle and preferences, while still ensuring long-term health and well-being.

>> Diet, exercise and weight loss

Many people exercise not just for their health, but because they want to lose weight. This terminology is in fact misleading, because what we weigh on the bathroom scales – our *body mass* – is a combination of both fat and *lean tissue*, which includes bone, muscles, ligaments and tendons. *Body composition* on the other hand is one of the key elements of fitness (see page 14), and may be defined as "the amount of body fat we carry relative to our lean tissue mass, expressed as a percentage."

It is generally considered healthy for a man to have a body fat percentage of 10–20%, and a woman, 15–25%. These figures are just a guide, though, and are influenced by many factors, including personal preferences, culture and tradition.

Determining your body fat percentage is also quite tricky to do. Common and accessible methods of measuring body fat – such as the body mass index,

If you have identified weight loss (reduced body fat) as a key goal in your boxing fitness program, we recommend that you base this on a *realistic appraisal of how you'd like to look and feel*. This is far preferable to aiming for a particular body composition or, indeed, weight on the scales. You may well find that as your boxing training tones your muscles, boosts your energy levels and gives you confidence, concerns about your weight become less important – or are alleviated altogether.

or BMI, which bases its calculations on your height and weight – all have their limitations, and results may fail to take account of such things as your natural body type and build. As discussed in more detail on page 14, the best way forward is probably to purchase a set of "body-fat scales" which, used properly, can give you reasonably accurate results.

Creating an "energy deficit"

Although we often agonize about it, losing body fat is based on a simple premise:

> We need to take in less energy – in other words, food – over the course of the day than we use up. This is known as creating an *energy deficit*.

Everything we do uses energy, even sleeping. So among other factors, the sum total of our energy requirements depends upon how active we are.

As a very rough guide, an average woman who is just going about her day needs to eat around 2000 calories to maintain a constant weight. For a man, this rises to around 2500 calories. If either of them wanted to lose body fat through diet alone, they would be advised to eat 250 calories less each day until their desired weight is reached.

Throw exercise into the mix, and things change. We can then create an energy deficit through training alone – by burning 250 calories more in our boxing fitness session than we would normally use during an average (non-exercising) day, while eating the same amount of food. Or we can do it through a combination of diet and exercise – in which case we could burn, say, 125 calories more through training, and eat 125 calories less than we would in a normal day.

The good news in all of this is that boxing fitness is high-intensity exercise, and thus uses up lots of calories. If you are careful with your diet, and try not to eat much more than usual – even though you may feel hungrier as a result of the exercise! – you will quickly notice a reduction in your body fat.

Don't overdo it

Be aware, though: if you create too large an energy deficit, your body will not have sufficient energy available to fuel your activities, or to sustain its internal processes. A healthy diet, with sufficient calories provided by all the key nutrient groups, will allow your muscles not only to work efficiently, but also to recover from and adapt positively to exercise.

If you under-eat, your body will think it is starving and tend to "hold on to" energy (fat) stores as an innate survival mechanism; this means that you will compromise positive changes in your body composition, even though you are training hard. Your general health and well-being will suffer, too, as your immune system is weakened and you become fatigued and susceptible to illness. Make sure you take in enough calories to sustain you.

You may need to experiment to find the optimal balance between "energy in" and "energy out," so be flexible and patient – it takes time. Obsessively counting calories and weighing yourself can be depressing and demotivating. Instead, enjoy your exercise and eat sensibly and healthily. If you do, success is just around the corner.

>> Hydration

We have already stressed the importance of drinking sufficient fluids to keep our bodies well hydrated. Water is lost from the body in urine production, as well as in the processes of breathing and sweating. But a range of other factors, such as environmental temperature, and of course exercise – which makes us breathe harder and sweat more – influences our individual hydration needs.

There are lots of different opinions as to how much water we should drink, most of them favoring around 8 average-sized glasses per day. Other sources go as far as advocating 2–3 litres; the American Institute of Medicine stipulates that men should drink about 13 cups of fluid daily, and women should drink 9. The truth is that it's almost impossible to generalize – and over-consumption can be as bad as under-consumption. Too much water can tax your kidneys, contribute to digestive disorders, and lead to mineral depletion and electrolyte imbalances.

As a guide, you are probably adequately hydrated if you rarely experience thirst, and your urine is colourless or slightly yellow. Signs of dehydration can include a dry mouth, headaches, light-headedness, dark or scanty urine, and constipation. Drinks containing caffeine or alcohol can increase fluid output (they are *diuretic*), and so make it more difficult to stay adequately hydrated.

>> Diet and alcohol

Alcohol is not classed as a nutrient, but the body can burn it as a source of energy. As well as being aware of the negative health implications of alcohol consumption, it's useful to know the following:

> Unlike carbohydrate, protein and fat – which pass through the stomach into the small intestine before being absorbed into the bloodstream – alcohol passes directly through the stomach's lining. It therefore arrives in the blood first, and will be used in preference to key nutrients, as fuel for the body's activities.

This means that while your body is using up the alcohol that is available in your bloodstream, the good-quality food that you have eaten as part of your balanced diet is being overlooked. Depending on how much alcohol you have consumed, these nutrients may be treated like any other form of excess energy, and either excreted or stored in your tissues as body fat. And this can continue for some time after you have stopped drinking – even into the following day!

Of course this doesn't mean that you shouldn't enjoy a glass or two of wine or a beer. After all, if you are eating well and exercising hard, it's great to be able to treat yourself. But keep in mind that if you're going to have a few drinks, it's advisable to keep an extra-close eye on what and how much you are eating around that 24-hour period.

Don't let all the sweat and fatigue of your boxing fitness program go to waste by jeopardizing your fitness gains for the sake of a boozy weekend. If you are in a dehydrated, hungover state, your training will suffer – not to mention the fact that you will feel awful while you're doing it. And you should never, ever exercise under the influence of alcohol: your techniques will be seriously compromised, and the risk of injury significantly increased.

> "
I like to go out drinking, especially when I'm at other people's gigs – obviously, I have to stay dry for my own. But since I started boxing training I've pretty much given up the booze. To be honest, it's not so much that I'm trying to be good and healthy; it's because when you step into the ring to work the focus pads, it is infinitely harder if you've been on the beers. It's just not worth the pain, and a waste of all the effort in any case. Somehow my instructor always knows if I've been drinking, and makes me pay for it!

Lawrence, 32
Musician

⓵③ Injury prevention and treatment

>> **Prevention is better than cure**

It is highly unlikely that you will get injured as a result of your boxing fitness training. If you follow the guidance given in Part Two and make sure that you are well prepared and organized for your sessions, you will minimize the chance of any mishaps occurring. Here is a brief recap of some sensible precautions that will keep you in one piece throughout your program.

❶ Choose a suitable training location. Although you can do a boxing fitness session almost anywhere, be sensible: only train in safe, well-lit places where you have plenty of room to manuever, and on an even floor-surface that precludes tripping or slipping hazards. Check for unexpected obstacles. Someone we know got tangled up with their dog, who thought the skipping rope would be great fun to play with.

❷ Show up to each session wearing appropriate clothing and footwear. Running shoes or boxing boots should support your ankles, so you don't turn them when engaged in footwork – and especially in the lateral lower-limb movements involved in boxing. Whatever footwear you choose, it should be sufficiently cushioned to absorb the impact of skipping, and afford a good grip via rubber soles – preventing you from slipping on flooring that may be, or become, wet with sweat or spilled water.

Avoid any loose or baggy clothing that might catch on or get snared up in a skipping rope, causing you to stumble or fall. Take the usual precautions with long hair, and remove any jewelery.

❸ Don't eat and train – but do drink enough. Don't eat while you are training; this includes chewing gum. People choke more than you might think from doing so.

❹ Bring water or other suitable fluids to every session, and drink little and often to ensure that you don't become dehydrated. Dehydration can make you lose focus and impair your co-ordination, making it more likely that you might injure yourself.

Wrap your hands well

As we have stressed, this is essential if you are including *any* punch bag or focus pad work in your program. Check back to pages 23–28 to remind yourself of the correct hand-wrapping technique.

Never be tempted simply to pull on bag or sparring gloves with no protection beneath. Even if your boxing gloves are good-quality, of supple leather and worn in, the vulnerable skin on your wrists and knuckles can chafe against the inside surface while you punch, causing blisters that can be problematic for some time afterwards. Hand-wraps also act as a gentle, supportive "splint" to your fingers and to the small bones in your hands and wrists, protecting them from repeated impact.

Warm up and cool down thoroughly

We have covered the importance of the warm-up in Chapter 4. If you come into your boxing session "cold," your muscles, tendons, ligaments and joints will be ill-prepared for the exercise to follow – making injury more likely.

Even if you don't actually injure yourself when training, without a good warm-up you will find that you are especially stiff and sore afterwards. Muscles in a tense, fatigued state are more prone to pulls and tears, even during normal daily activity. It's not worth the risk.

At the end of your session, do a five-minute cool-down to bring your muscles back to their pre-training state. You can repeat the static stretches you performed prior to your session, or include some new ones for variety. Concentrate on those muscles or muscle groups you have worked the hardest. For example, if you have done a lot of punching, perform more stretches for your shoulders, chest and back – although of course you should not neglect the lower body (see pages 37–42 for exercises and techniques); a ratio of 2 : 1 is a good guide. If footwork has been the focus of the session, reverse the ratio.

Avoid getting cold after training, by toweling off any sweat and quickly putting on some dry clothes. A hot bath or shower is beneficial, too.

>> Work on your technique

In addition to being properly prepared and organized for training, work hard to perfect your boxing techniques. Good technique is fundamental to injury prevention. For example, ensure that you always punch with a strong wrist; if you don't, your hand may bend over as it makes contact with the bag or

Getting your technique right can prevent injuries – in this case, the correct position of the elbow for a right hook focus pad. Even if your wrist isn't actually injured, repeated bending of it when punching can, over time, cause pain and problems.

So read about the techniques in Part Three and recap regularly on your stance, how to punch, and footwork. Where possible, train in front of a mirror to check your own posture and form, and ask others to watch and comment on your training if and when appropriate. Expert advice is invaluable in this respect. Even the most seasoned professional boxers continue to hone and improve on technical skills throughout their careers.

>> Potential injuries

As with any sport or workout, we can't predict and prevent every possible injury. However, what follows are the injuries you are most likely to encounter doing boxing-related training.

Remember: if you experience any undue pain and soreness during your boxing fitness session, it's best to stop what you're doing and rest. Always seek medical advice if the problem persists or worsens, or if you are concerned. Only resume training when the affected area is trouble-free, and do so gradually and sensibly.

Soft tissue injury

Boxing fitness is a safe, non-contact type of training so injuries or ailments tend to be restricted to minor soft-tissue injuries and inflammation – affecting muscles, tendons and fascia, rather than bones or joints. When such problems do occur, they are most likely to affect the arms, wrists and hands as a result of repeated punching against a resistant surface (the heavy bag or focus pads). Incorrect or poor punching technique can cause or exacerbate the condition.

If you get sore shoulders, hands or wrists, stop training and rest in order to prevent further pain and inflammation. Ice the affected area to reduce the inflammatory response. Place the ice in a towel

before applying it, to protect your skin. A bag of frozen peas works wonders.

If the affected area swells up, compression is recommended. Use an elastic bandage to maintain healthy blood flow in the limb; the bandage should fit snugly but not be too tight. Finally, elevate the limb to limit swelling and to aid the removal of waste products from the problem area.

RICE (REST, ICE, COMPRESSION, ELEVATION)
This is a useful way of remembering this treatment combination. Resume training cautiously as soon as you are pain-free.

Blisters

As we have said, chafing and blisters can occur when the delicate skin on your hands, and especially over your knuckles, is subjected to repeated friction. It's best if possible to avoid this; once the skin is broken, you will need to wait for it to heal before resuming training.

Prevent blisters by wrapping your hands well, and by working out on a punching bag that is not too "tight" or firm. Choose leather gloves where possible, and wear them in gradually over time so that the leather becomes supple with lots of give. You can also bind half an ordinary, unused bathroom sponge over your knuckles on each hand, underneath the hand-wraps, to provide extra cushioning.

If your skin does start to get sore, take a break from the punching bag and focus pad work, and concentrate for a while on the speed ball or shadow boxing until it subsides. In time, the skin will toughen up and, depending on how much and how hard you punch, calluses may form. These can be unsightly but do protect you from further problems.

Don't continue punching if blisters have developed and the skin is broken or bleeding. Keep the affected area clean and dry. There is conflicting advice as to whether or not you should wear adhesive bandages to promote healing and prevent infection; we recommend that you do – but if you are unsure or concerned, consult your doctor for advice.

Pain from skipping

This can sometimes occur in the feet, ankles and knees because skipping is a high-impact activity. As we have advised, wear well-cushioned running shoes rather than boxing boots, and skip on a floor-surface that is neither unyielding nor over-soft or unstable.

If such precautions don't prevent or help with pain in the affected limb, limit your skipping to short, light intervals – perhaps 30 seconds at a time, with a minute's rest in-between, three times per session. Then gradually build this up. In the worst-case scenario, you may have to stop skipping altogether – but you can always work on your stamina with alternative cardio-based activities, or on your speed, balance and co-ordination with lots of footwork and quick punching combinations.

Even if you decide to omit skipping from your program for now, try it again from time to time. You may well find that as you progress with your training, the structures surrounding and supporting your feet, ankles and knees become stronger, so that the pain no longer occurs.

Delayed onset muscle soreness (DOMS) is the term applied to stiffness felt in your muscles in the days after hard or unaccustomed exercise. DOMS can be quite severe. It may begin within 24 hours post-workout, but is often felt more intensely 48–72 hours later. The syndrome is thought to occur as a result of microscopic damage to the muscle fibers – but don't worry, this is perfectly normal! When the same type of exercise is repeated next time, a positive adaptation occurs in the muscles to prevent further problems. If you are new to boxing fitness, you are likely to experience some DOMS, especially in your chest, shoulders and upper back. Unless the pain persists and you are concerned – in which case, consult your doctor – it's a case of grin and bear it as you shape up to become a seasoned champ.

14 Health matters

This chapter touches on special considerations for people who may want to participate in boxing fitness training, but are:

> Under 18 years of age
> A more mature or elderly practitioner
> Pregnant or have recently given birth

In addition, those who have been diagnosed with a pre-existing disease or condition, such as heart disease, diabetes or asthma, may also need to take certain precautions to ensure that they remain safe and well while training.

> While we have made every effort to include practical, useful information on these topics, it is not within the scope of this book to address all health matters in comprehensive detail. If you have questions or concerns that are not covered here, it's important that you seek professional advice – *before* embarking on a boxing fitness program – from a qualified medical or nutritional expert.

>> Children and young adults

Children and young adults can benefit hugely from boxing fitness training. Not only do they find it enjoyable, but it also gives them a safe and controlled environment in which to use up their energy, and channel any anger or frustration they may be feeling.

Learning how to "handle oneself" is an important part of every child's development. Boxing, as a sport and as a fitness activity, is an ideal way in which to teach them the discipline, focus and self-control they will need in their daily lives.

Since health and well-being are so closely interlinked, there is a further, relevant dimension to this. For many young adults today, boxing clubs and gyms offer opportunities for sporting and social inclusion that may not exist for them elsewhere. It has been shown that young people who are harder-to-reach through more mainstream channels, who may have dropped out of the education system, and who are therefore vulnerable and at risk of turning to crime or violence, welcome boxing as a physical and emotional outlet.

From the age of 11, children have the option of training to compete in the sport of boxing – which, in America, falls under the auspices of USA Boxing (usaboxing.org/). Other national governing bodies and local/regional divisions can be contacted via the International Boxing Association (www.aiba.org). Amateur boxers wear protective headgear, and the sport is subject to stringent safety measures to protect its participants.

If your child wishes to join an amateur boxing club, check to make sure that the club is fully affiliated to the appropriate divisional arm of the sport's governing body; and that the rules and regulations are carefully adhered to by the coaches and management. It is your responsibility, as well as that of the club, to protect your child's health, safety and welfare during training and competition. See page 161–4 for more information.

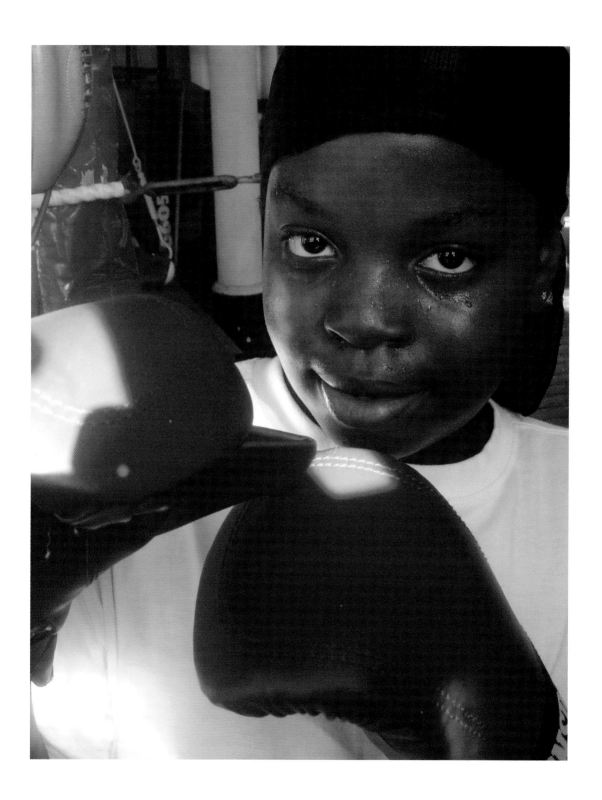

As long as a young person is generally fit and healthy, there is nothing stopping them from embarking on a full boxing fitness program. The benefits they gain will be wide-ranging, and are both physical – especially in respect of addressing a rising trend in youth obesity – and psychological. Boxing training has been shown to increase confidence and self-esteem in the face of bullying behavior at school.

Although there are no contraindications to exercise for most healthy children, the lifting of heavy weights should be avoided until an individual has reached his or her full growth potential. Any resistance work undertaken as part of a conditioning program should be limited to the young person's bodyweight: bones, muscles and joints in the growing body must not be put under undue stress if they are to develop fully and healthily.

>> The older practitioner

As we get older, we are more likely to contract a number of diseases associated with the aging process. These include:

> Cardiovascular diseases such as coronary heart disease and high blood pressure

> Musculoskeletal diseases like osteoporosis (brittle bones) and certain types of arthritis

> Respiratory diseases such as asthma

> Metabolic diseases including diabetes and obesity

> Neurological diseases like Parkinson's and Alzheimer's

Even if we do not suffer from any of these conditions, certain negative changes in a person's anatomy and

physiology are unavoidable as we age – such as loss of bone density, decreased range of movement in the joints, increased body fat, and a decline in postural control. For these and other reasons, it's highly recommended that an older adult (from the age of 50 upwards) seek clearance and advice from a qualified medical professional before embarking on any unaccustomed exercise program. If you are aged 50 or over, and are new to boxing fitness, this certainly applies to you.

Most people will simply be given a quick check-up and, if there are no health indications to the contrary, be encouraged to maintain a good level of physical activity – or even to increase this in a safe and sensible way. The benefits of exercise described on page 4 are equally, if not more, relevant to us as we age. They include:

> reduced body fat and increased lean tissue mass

> increased bone and muscle strength

> improved mobility, posture and balance

> enhanced cardiorespiratory function

> emotional and mental well-being

Osteoporosis – or loss of bone density – is particularly relevant to women. We all experience loss of bone strength from the age of about 30, but women are more susceptible due to the relative size of their bones and changes in their hormones. By the time a woman reaches 70, the National Osteoporosis Society estimates that she will have lost 30% of her bone density and will be at risk of fractures and breaks, even when doing normal day-to-day activities.

The good news is that regular weight-bearing activity can slow down this loss of bone strength. The more you do, the stronger your bones grow, and the less likely you are to suffer the ill effects of brittle bones. In this case prevention really is better than cure, and a regular regimen of boxing fitness training – or any other kind of weight-bearing activity – can help prevent the development of this disease.

So don't assume that your activity levels should be lower as you get older, or that once you hit 40 your body is doomed to a decline you can neither slow down nor prevent! Take expert advice; follow any recommended precautions individual to your state of health; and enjoy your exercise sessions for a long time to come.

>> Other conditions

People can enjoy boxing fitness training despite suffering from conditions such as asthma and diabetes. It is important to make a full and frank assessment of your own medical condition, to consult your doctor if you are in doubt about the suitability of your training, and to make sure that someone at the gym is aware of your health requirements. Although it can be tempting to push yourself hard in boxing fitness training, it is advisable to start gently and to listen to your body's response. Only you can know how you are feeling and coping with the training, and it's your responsibility to pace yourself accordingly.

When consulting your doctor, it's a good idea to take this book along with you. He or she can then have a quick look at the type of activities involved in boxing training, and take into account its particular set of physical demands when screening you.

If you're given the OK to train, it is recommended that you increase the warm-up and cool-down periods, and include more mobility exercises to help lubricate your joints.

If you work out with a qualified personal trainer, or train at a boxing gym or health club, you will be required to complete a health questionnaire (sometimes known as a Physical Activity Readiness Questionnaire, or 'PAR-Q') before you do your first session.

Make sure you answer the questions honestly; they're for your own safety and well-being. And don't be offended if you are asked to provide a doctor's note as proof of your fitness to train: the instructor or company has certain legal and ethical considerations to comply with, to the benefit of everyone involved.

> ### ALWAYS REMEMBER!
>
> Before undertaking any unaccustomed activity, and especially something as energetic as boxing fitness, advice must always be sought from a qualified medical professional. Follow their guidance to ensure your own safety and well-being before, during and after training.

>> Pregnancy and post-pregnancy

If you have been generally fit and active prior to your pregnancy, and everything is going as planned, there is no reason why you shouldn't either begin or continue a boxing fitness program – albeit with certain modifications (see below) – for as long as you feel up to it.

In fact, exercise of an appropriate type and level is positively recommended in pregnancy, to keep you in shape both physically and mentally. Whether you are new to boxing training, or a more seasoned practitioner, your sessions will help to:

> burn off excess calories, making the job of post-labor slimming and toning much easier

> develop your cardiovascular system, improving blood flow and thus alleviating some typical pregnancy-related discomforts, such as swollen ankles

> enhance muscular strength and endurance – reducing physical fatigue while carrying your baby, aiding the birth process, and making you stronger for those tiring times when you are caring for your newborn

> increase your endorphin levels, alleviating any stress, insomnia or anxiety you may be feeling

> boost your confidence, as you look and feel healthier and happier with that enviable maternal "glow!"

Some sensible precautions

When your pregnancy is detected, speak to your doctor about your desire to stay fit and active, and listen to his or her advice. As well as scheduling regular check-ups, especially with regard to your blood pressure, they are likely to warn against any impactful activity – so drop the skipping element of your sessions and replace with more core stability exercises (see pages 139–47), which will help you maintain good posture as your bump grows.

Adequate hydration is very important for you and your unborn baby, so remember to sip water little and often, before, during and after your sessions. Wear sensible, supportive running shoes and layers of thin clothing so you can avoid overheating or becoming chilled. Most importantly, *listen to your body* and don't push yourself beyond what you feel able to achieve. If you experience any faintness, dizziness, pain or other worrying symptoms, stop what you're doing right away, and seek medical advice.

During pregnancy, to prepare for the birth process, your body produces increased levels of a hormone called *relaxin*. These levels remain elevated for at least three months after your baby is delivered, and longer if you are breastfeeding. Relaxin has the effect of increasing the elasticity of ligaments and cartilage, leading to potential joint instability. So to avoid any damage to your joints, take good care when stretching (see pages 35–42) to keep the position within the normal range of movement, and check your posture and technique throughout.

This section of the book details specific training sessions for you to follow, and suggests ways in which you can progress your boxing fitness going forward – depending on your individual goals.

>> Be patient

By now you will have clearly identified your goals, and hopefully you will have made time and space in your life to address them. It can't be stressed enough that, while boxing training is a highly effective and fun way of getting into shape, you must be patient as you work through your program. Nothing good ever comes easily, and fitness is no exception.

There will be times when you feel tired and frustrated. And there will be days on which your boxing session leaves you energized, confident, able to cope with anything that life may throw at you. Your clothes fit better; you hold your head higher; people comment on how great you look. Those days make all the hard work worthwhile.

>> Be flexible

A full boxing fitness program requires access to a range of equipment and facilities (see Part Two). But you can start with much less: the minimum you need in order to participate is:

> a pair of hand-wraps
> a skipping rope
> a way of timing yourself over the course of rounds and rest periods.

If you are able to purchase or use a punching bag and a pair of boxing gloves, this adds a further dimension to your workout, with more ways of challenging yourself and more variety to enjoy. Find a qualified instructor to hold the focus pads, and you are doing everything a boxer does, bar the person-to-person contact – and benefiting proportionally.

Bear in mind that *you* are the boss of your own training program. As long as you observe sensible safety precautions, and follow the technical guidance given in this book, there's nothing to prevent you from devising different and exciting ways to put together your boxing fitness sessions.

So explore all your options, and consider the importance of what you are investing in: your health, fitness and well-being. You may find that with a little more time, effort and outlay, you can significantly extend the impact of your boxing fitness program.

Of course, it may still be that some of the individual training elements remain unavailable to you, for reasons of cost, access or medical constraints. In the following pages we cover some of these eventualities, by suggesting practical alternatives to the traditional boxing techniques. In this way you can be as flexible as the workout itself, and therefore find fewer reasons to delay or avoid exercising altogether.

"

I started boxing training after a long period of on-again, off-again gym membership – due mainly to pressures at work. I got into it straight away, and within a few weeks could manage three rounds of all the techniques. But I'd already booked a fortnight's holiday and the resort didn't have a gym. In the past I would have just shrugged and said, OK. But this time I took my hand-wraps, skipping rope and interval timer. Every evening I shadow-boxed on the beach as the sun was setting . . . and some other people even joined in!

Nicola, 34
Accountant

"

>> How to use this section

For all the sessions detailed here, it is assumed that:

> You have read and fully understood Parts One to Four of the book.

> You are in general good health, or have received clearance by your doctor to undertake a boxing fitness program.

> You will listen to your body. That may sound strange, but while this book (and an instructor, if you have one) can help guide you toward your goals, only one person knows how you really feel – and that's you. Some days you will know instinctively that you can push yourself; on others, your body may tell you to take it easy. Be sensitive to that, and communicate how you are feeling honestly with any others involved in your program. Don't beat yourself up for a "bad" session: put it behind you, and come back fighting tomorrow.

Choose the right training level

To safeguard your physical and emotional well-being, it's important that you be realistic about your expectations. This means choosing a training level that is suitable for you now, at this time in your life – not for the person you were a few years ago, or the person you'd like to be if only things were different!

Being realistic about your current abilities and future potential will ensure that you enjoy your exercise sessions, and achieve measurable fitness gains, leaving you feeling positive and encouraged.

If you begin with a session that is too advanced, you risk becoming over-fatigued and very quickly discouraged – and you may even give up. Too easy, and you can become bored and disillusioned. Both possibilities set you up to fail, so to help you judge where you should pitch your boxing fitness sessions, each workout in this section specifies whether it is aimed primarily at *novice*, *intermediate* or *advanced* practitioners. We define each level as follows.

> ### Novice

This applies to you if you are new to boxing fitness training, or new to exercise. Alternatively, you have a basic level of fitness gained through being physically active in your daily life, or through irregular/low-key participation in other sports or gym workouts.

> ### Intermediate

As an intermediate practitioner, you may already have tried boxing training or another combat-based activity such as mixed martial arts over a sustained period of time. You consider yourself to possess a good level of fitness, perhaps gained through regular participation in other sports or gym-based workouts.

> ### Advanced

If you are an advanced practitioner, you may have significant experience of boxing training or another combat-based activity. Alternatively – or in addition – you may have been in regular attendance at a gym or health club over a sustained period of time; or be an athlete with a high level of general and sports-specific fitness.

Of course, you will not jump suddenly from one level to the next, but *build your training up gradually*. Use the sessions detailed in this section as a guide to what to aim for, as you move from being new or relatively new to boxing fitness, to being an experienced old-hand, skipping double-unders and confounding people with your lightning-quick combinations!

Progressing within a given training session

> ### Keep the activities in sequence

Once you have chosen the best "entry level" session for you, work through the activities in the correct sequence: there are good reasons for the way in which they are ordered. For example, shadow boxing serves as an extension of the dynamic warm-up, enabling you to rehearse boxing-specific movements before the resistance of the punching bag is introduced. Skipping emphasizes the lower body, so it splits up punching bag and focus pad work and gives your upper body a bit of a rest.

> **Manage your rounds**

For each of the activities, keep the three-minute round in mind – but if you need to break each round down into more manageable intervals, that's fine. Feel your way. If you are completely new to exercise, you may wish to try 30-second efforts with a 30-second rest between each. After a few sessions, when this starts to become easier, you might cut down your rest periods to 15 seconds … or increase your effort intervals to a minute. It's up to you.

As your fitness improves and you start to feel more comfortable with the techniques, you will keep going for longer without a break. Eventually you will be able to perform each activity over three minutes without stopping, which is a great feeling. But even though you can shadow box, skip, or punch the bag for a whole round, remember that there are other rounds to follow! Pace yourself carefully, and be sure to reinforce your progress until you are confident that you can complete the full session as specified, and reasonably comfortably, before considering a move upwards.

> **Make the most of your recovery time**

However you manage your rounds, take a full minute's rest between each – no matter what activity you are undertaking. If you skimp on your recovery, rounds will become progressively harder and your technique may suffer, so time your rest periods properly.

Spend the minute between rounds towelling down and sipping some water. You will cool off quickly when you stop working and the sweat begins to evaporate from your skin. For this reason, consider putting on an additional, dry layer of clothing and removing it again before the next round.

During recovery periods, we suggest that you walk around rather than sitting down, so that your muscles don't stiffen up. It can also help to focus on getting your breathing back under control as your mind prepares for the next three-minute effort.

Moving to the next level

> **It's personal**

Judging when to increase the difficulty of your sessions is tricky, because everyone progresses at different rates – and each person's situation and lifestyle are highly individual. Remember too that within any given session, there is a range of techniques to learn, practice and master. The rate at which you will do this depends on many factors, perhaps most significantly your cardiovascular fitness and muscular endurance (see pages 13 and 14).

For example, if you are new to skipping but your fitness level is intermediate, you may be able to get through a whole round of repeated efforts – albeit with a lot of stumbling and muttering. It will take someone who is new to skipping *and* new to exercise a lot longer to persevere continuously over the full three minutes.

And other factors come into play, like how many times a week you are able to exercise. Ideally you will fit in three sessions a week, in which case you will progress through the sessions and levels more quickly than if you're working out twice. This is *not* to say that you won't make good fitness gains with two workouts a week! Just that you should fully consider your own situation, and have realistic expectations about meeting the goals you have set for yourself.

> **Keep a record**

To monitor your progress against your stated fitness goals, it can really help to keep a record of your sessions – together with a commentary on how you felt before, during and after them. You can do this with a simple journal, jotting down some or all of the following:

> The date and the time of day you are working out (you may review your journal and discover that it suits you much better to exercise in the morning, or in the evening, and so on).

> Whether/what you have eaten and drank beforehand (and if this is usual or unusual; for example, if you get a stitch while training, it can be caused by eating or drinking too soon and/or too much before your workout – so you can learn from this).

> The particular session you are undertaking (whether it is at novice, intermediate or ad-

vanced level; be sure also to detail the number of rounds for each activity, with the effort and rest intervals you are splitting them into, if relevant).

> Your weight, if reducing body fat is one of your key fitness goals (to ensure an accurate result, weigh yourself on the same set of scales every time, in just your underwear and with bare feet; also take into account what you may have eaten or drank beforehand, which can make quite a difference).

> How you felt before, during and after the session (physically and emotionally, good and bad – and if you can pin down the cause of any of those feelings, if they are significantly different from your normal state: e.g. fatigue from a late night; poor focus from a bad day at work; great energy levels from an improved diet, and so on).

Devise a personal record *according to how useful the information is to you*, when you look back over it to check your progress. We tend to live in the moment, so if we have a difficult day culminating in a difficult session, this can be very discouraging. But if your journal proves that even though you're feeling low, you've actually been training well and positively for several days or even weeks, it helps to restore an accurate perspective. That perspective can make the difference between success and failure – because without it, you may give up. So if possible, keep a training diary.

> **Build up gradually**

In the following pages, we describe detailed sessions for three training levels: novice, intermediate, and advanced. The main difference between the sessions is *the duration* – how long the whole session lasts – which increases exponentially as you get fitter, and more rounds are added for each of the boxing fitness techniques. But there are other ways of varying and building on your workouts, and we suggest some of these on page 150.

Of course, you will not leap from level to level, but rather build up gradually until you have achieved and are comfortable with one level before proceeding to the next. As we have said, the rate at which you get to this point depends on many factors – so it's only possible to give a broad idea, based on our experience, of the time it will take someone to move from novice, to intermediate, to advanced practitioner.

The following guidelines assume that you are training three times per week; if such frequency is impractical, your fitness gains will be a little slower, so allow for this.

> If you are in full health but new to regular exercise in general, and to boxing fitness in particular, you can expect to spend *between four and six weeks* getting comfortable with the novice-level session as described on page 108. You should notice a boost in your energy levels, and, if you are eating healthily and sleeping well, this may well be accompanied by other positive signs such as gradual weight loss and improved posture and muscle tone.

> The timeframe may shrink if your base fitness level is good; however, you still need to take a while to learn, practice and master unfamiliar techniques. This learning phase is in many ways the most important stage in your whole exercise program. If you take it slowly and pay due care and attention to each training element, you will progress from a position of knowledge and power. Don't rush things, or cut corners – it will compromise your achievements and is really not worth it in the end.

> When you are comfortable with the novice-level workout, and can complete each part of it with relative ease and confidence (keeping in mind that it's never "easy"!), you should be able to build up your training sufficiently to complete an intermediate-level session *within six weeks to three months*.

> At this stage, you should really notice a positive difference in many aspects of your daily life. So persevere! We're willing to bet that people start commenting on your appearance – if they haven't done so already. If you are maintaining a sensible diet, resting between sessions and getting some early nights, you will be shedding body fat and improving overall toning. Enhanced confidence and self-esteem will be shining through. You're training like a boxer now: good for you.

> There is likely to be a longer gap before you are ready to take on an advanced-level session: perhaps *a further three to six months*. A typical session at this level comprises six full rounds of each boxing fitness technique, and the total duration can be up to an hour and a half.

> Advanced boxing fitness is hard, challenging training, requiring mental focus and determination as well as sustained physical effort. If we make it sound a little intimidating, that's only because we want you to be thoroughly and properly prepared. When you are, few workouts are more guaranteed to get you into the shape of your life. By now, we believe that you will be "hooked" on boxing training, incorporating it into your life on an ongoing basis, and enjoying all the benefits it can bestow upon your mind and your body.

Don't rush to move up a level in your boxing fitness program; it may take some time for you to advance from one level to the next. Only add rounds if you are confident that you have mastered the basic techniques involved, and can complete the number of three-minute efforts specified in the session you are working on.

>> Boxing circuit training

Finally in this section, we include information about the boxing circuit – a great addition to your training repertoire. The full circuit takes an hour, so can comprise a whole session, but you can cut it down and use an abbreviated version as an effective alternative to another boxing fitness technique. The circuit is also very flexible, so that versions of it may be undertaken at any fitness level. It is described in detail on pages 129–36.

Our boxing circuit is unique, because it has been designed specifically around the concept of the three-minute round with one minute's recovery. You carry out a set of six exercises in sequence, all of which have been selected to strengthen and tone the major muscles involved in boxing training. When combined over set time periods with specific rests, these exercises are also highly effective in improving your stamina – so that when you're working on your boxing fitness techniques, you can persevere for longer and recover more quickly.

BOXING FITNESS SESSION 1: NOVICE LEVEL

DURATION: 1 HOUR

*This session assumes that you have access to the full range of personal equipment listed in **Part Two**.
Alternatives to some of the techniques are suggested in Session 5 on pages 125–77.*

Minutes/Rounds	Activity (equipment needed)	Page ref.	Comments
5 minutes	Wrap your hands (hand-wraps)	23	Do this before every boxing fitness session. Protects your hands inside boxing gloves; encourages a "professional" and focused attitude; and helps keep your hands in the correct position as you make a fist.
10 minutes	Warm-up: "pulse-raiser"	35	Light cardiovascular exercise. Raises your heart rate; lubricates your joints; and increases the elasticity of your muscles. Suitable activities include jogging or cycling; or in the gym, treadmill, step, cross-trainer or exercise bike – choose one of these activities for your pulse-raiser, and try to vary your choice from session to session.
	Warm-up: static stretches	37	Increases range of motion of joints; may decrease the likelihood of injury/post-session stiffness. Include at least one stretch for each of the following: neck, shoulders, chest, upper back, lower back, waist, front of thighs, back of thighs, calves, ankles. Enter into stretch gently, hold each stretch for 10–15 seconds, and do not bounce. Maintain good posture; add variety to avoid staleness.
	Warm-up: dynamic stretches	41	Sport-specific movements designed to mobilize your joints and prepare your body for boxing training. Try those recommended on page 41, or research/design your own. Replicate boxing movements: e.g. rotational (hips, torso, shoulders, for punching), and squatting (stance and footwork).

Minutes/Rounds	Activity (equipment needed)	Page ref.	Comments
• 2 x 3-minute rounds • 1 x minute's rest between rounds *Total 8 minutes* If necessary, split each round into manageable efforts: e.g. 30 seconds on, 15 seconds off. Keep efforts and rest intervals regular, and build on these to progress. *Always take one full minute's rest between rounds.*	Shadow boxing (*hand-wraps*)	64	For cardiovascular fitness; muscular endurance; technical rehearsal; speed, balance and co-ordination; psychological benefits (focus, discipline). Practice individual punches, combinations, defensive/evasive techniques, and footwork. Ideally perform all, or in part, in front of a mirror, to monitor form and provide a "shadow" opponent. Below is an example of how you might structure your two rounds of shadow boxing, but we encourage you to be creative and try out lots of different ideas of your own. Always take a full minute's rest between rounds. **Round 1 comprises:** • 1 minute of jabs and crosses (rehearse single jabs, double jabs, double-jab cross, one-two, one-two-three, four straight) *followed by* • 1 minute of hooks and hook combinations (rehearse single hooks, double hooks, jab-hook-cross, jab-double hook-cross, double jab-hook-cross) *followed by* • 1 minute of uppercuts and uppercut combinations (rehearse front and rear hand uppercuts, jab-uppercut-cross, jab-double uppercut-cross, continuous alternating uppercuts) **Round 2 comprises:** • 1 minute spent rehearsing your footwork, with your guard up and no punches thrown (move in different directions, bounce "in and out" on your toes, circle an imaginary opponent, "roll" back and forwardas if evading counterpunches) *followed by* • 1 minute of evasive/defensive techniques (slipping, bobbing and weaving, and counterpunching in response to imagined shots from an opponent) *followed by* • 1 minute of continual punching, footwork and evasive/defensive techniques combined

Minutes/Rounds	Activity (equipment needed)	Page ref.	Comments
• 2 x 3-minute rounds • 1 x minute's rest between rounds *Total 8 minutes* If necessary, split each round into manageable efforts: e.g. 30 seconds on, 15 seconds off. Keep efforts and rest intervals regular, and build on these to progress. *Always take one full minute's rest between rounds.*	Punching bag (*hand-wraps beneath bag or sparring gloves*)	70	Provides resistance to punches and encourages reflexive, mobile response. For cardiovascular fitness; muscular endurance; strength/power; speed; technical rehearsal; psychological benefits (including channeling aggression). Practice individual punches, combinations, defensive/evasive techniques, and footwork. Here are a few examples of how you might work the bag over a 3-minute period, but you can devise your own. (Use your imagination, keep it at a pace and complexity suitable to your fitness level, and remember to take a full minute's rest between the rounds): • 3 minutes of jabs and crosses (rehearse single jabs, double jabs, double-jab cross, one-two, one-two-three, four straight; vary your speed and the power of your punches) • 3 minutes of hooks and hook combinations (rehearse single hooks, double hooks, jab-hook-cross, jab-double hook-cross, double jab-hook-cross; vary your speed and the power of your punches) • 3 minutes on the uppercut bag, practicing uppercuts and uppercut combinations (e.g. 10 x front hand uppercut; 10 by back hand uppercut; alternating front and back hand uppercuts; do this at speed; do this with maximum power) • 3 minutes rehearsing your footwork, with your guard up and throwing only jabs and double jabs between movements (work around the bag in different directions; bounce "in and out" on your toes, throwing some sharp jabs on the "in" movement; push the bag so that it swings and then duck, slip, and bob and weave to avoid it; add some counterpunches) • 3 x 1 minute of continual punching with 10 seconds rest between minutes

Minutes/Rounds	Activity (equipment needed)	Page ref.	Comments
• 2 x 3-minute rounds • 1 x minute's rest between rounds *Total 8 minutes* If necessary, split each round into manageable efforts: e.g. 30 seconds on, 15 seconds off. Keep efforts and rest intervals regular, and build on these to progress. *Always take one full minute's rest between rounds.*	Skipping (*skipping rope*)	66	For cardiovascular fitness; muscular endurance; speed, balance and co-ordination; psychological benefits (focus, discipline). Master the basic two-footed technique and/or "running in place." Then vary techniques and routines for progression. This is an impact activity: wear cushioned footwear and use a "giving" floor-surface.
• 1 x 3-minute round • 1 x minute's rest *Total 4 minutes*	Focus pads (*hand-wraps beneath bag or sparring gloves*)	75	Addresses every aspect of boxing training – comprehensive boxing fitness workout. Perform only with a qualified instructor. The more imagination your trainer applies to your focus pad work, the more enjoyable it will be, so track down an experienced and skilled practitioner who can be creative with the pads. He or she may ask you to perform any or all of the following combinations, in sequence or mixed-up, and incorporate footwork together with defensive/evasive techniques: • jab, double jab, double jab-cross • one-two, one-two-three, four straight • one-two hook, one-two-double hook-cross

Minutes/Rounds	Activity (equipment needed)	Page ref.	Comments
			• one-two-uppercut, one-two-three-uppercut, one-two-double uppercut-cross • jab to the head, jab to the body, cross • ducking, slipping, bobbing and weaving • footwork, such as rolling forward/backward while or after punching, lateral steps followed by punches and combinations, bouncing in and out and throwing sharp jabs on the "in" movement
6 minutes	Non-boxing cardio activity (various; see Comments)	n/a	Further improves cardiovascular fitness and muscular endurance; enhances recovery between rounds; speeds body fat reduction. Suitable activities include jogging and cycling; or gym machines such as stepper, cross-trainer, exercise bike, treadmill. Choose one activity per session, and vary from session to session if possible.
5 minutes	Core training (mat or towel; Swiss ball, medicine ball) **OR** Resistance training (mat; other – e.g. dumbbells) **OR** A combination of core and resistance training (mat; other – varies)	139 148	Strengthens abdominal and other core muscles. Improves posture, and has beneficial effect on boxing techniques. Strengthens specific muscles or muscle groups. Improves muscular endurance and encourages body fat reduction. Improves posture, and has beneficial effect on boxing techniques. You can perform your core and resistance exercises either in groups of repetitions (single efforts), or over set intervals (time periods). Here are a couple of examples of how you might structure your core/resistance work – but as always, we encourage you to come up with your own, creative ideas: **Combination 1 (core):** • 30 seconds basic abdominal crunch, 15 seconds rest • 15 seconds long lever abdominal crunch, 15 seconds rest • 15 seconds front plank, 15 seconds rest • 15 seconds back extensions (arms by sides), 15 seconds rest

Minutes/Rounds	Activity (equipment needed)	Page ref.	Comments
			• 15 seconds back extensions (arms stretched out in front), 15 seconds rest • 15 seconds left-side plank, 15 seconds rest • 15 seconds right-side plank, 15 seconds rest • 15 seconds ski sit, 15 seconds rest • 15 seconds bicycle abdominal crunch, 15 seconds rest **Combination 2 (resistance):** • 3 x 10 bodyweight squats, 15 seconds rest between sets • 3 x 10 push-ups or wall push-ups, 15 seconds rest between sets • 10 dumbbell right-side lunge, 10 dumbbell left-side lunge, 15 seconds rest; repeat x 2 • 10 triceps dips, 10 biceps curl; repeat x 2
5 minutes	Cool-down	35	Encourages the body to return gradually to its pre-exercise state. Perform gentle, static stretches for each part of the body. Remove wet clothing from next to the skin, and put on dry layers.

NB: Always take water to your session; sip little and often.

BOXING FITNESS SESSION 2: INTERMEDIATE LEVEL

DURATION: 1 HOUR 15 MINUTES

This session assumes that you have access to the full range of personal equipment listed in Part Two. Alternatives to some of the techniques are suggested in Session 5 on page 125.

Minutes/Rounds	Activity (equipment needed)	Page ref.	Comments
5 minutes	Wrap your hands (hand-wraps)	23	Do this before every boxing fitness session. Protects your hands inside boxing gloves; encourages a "professional" and focused attitude; and helps keep your hands in the correct position as you make a fist.
10 minutes	Warm-up: "pulse-raiser"	35	Light cardiovascular exercise. Raises your heart rate; lubricates your joints; and increases the elasticity of your muscles. Suitable activities include jogging or cycling; or in the gym, treadmill, step, cross-trainer or exercise bike – choose one of these activities for your pulse-raiser, and try to vary your choice from session to session.
	Warm-up: static stretches	37	Increases range of motion of joints; may decrease the likelihood of injury and post-session stiffness. Include at least one stretch for each of the following: neck, shoulders, chest, upper back, lower back, waist, front of thighs, back of thighs, calves, ankles. Enter into stretch gently, hold each stretch for 10-15 seconds, and do not bounce. Maintain good posture; add variety.
	Warm-up: dynamic stretches	41	Sport-specific movements designed to mobilize your joints and prepare your body for boxing training. Try those recommended on page 41, or research/design your own. Replicate boxing movements: e.g. rotational (hips, torso, shoulders, for punching), and squatting (stance and footwork).

Minutes/Rounds	Activity (equipment needed)	Page ref.	Comments
• 3 x 3-minute rounds • 1 x minute's rest between rounds *Total 12 minutes* If necessary, split each round into manageable efforts: e.g. 60 seconds on, 15 seconds off. Keep efforts and rest intervals regular, and build on these to progress. *Always take one full minute's rest between rounds.*	Shadow boxing *(hand-wraps)*	64	For cardiovascular fitness; muscular endurance; technical rehearsal; speed, balance and co-ordination; psychological benefits (focus, discipline). Practice individual punches, combinations, defensive/evasive techniques, and footwork. Ideally perform all, or in part, in front of a mirror, to monitor form and provide a "shadow" opponent. *See Session 1 for some ideas about how you might structure your rounds of shadow boxing.*
• 3 x 3-minute rounds • 1 x minute's rest between rounds *Total 12 minutes*	Punching bag *(hand-wraps beneath bag or sparring gloves)*	70	Provides resistance to punches and encourages reflexive, mobile response. For cardiovascular fitness; muscular endurance; strength/power; speed; technical rehearsal; psychological benefits (including channeling aggression). Practice individual punches, combinations, defensive/evasive techniques, and footwork.

Minutes/Rounds	Activity (equipment needed)	Page ref.	Comments
If necessary, split each round into manageable efforts: e.g. 60 seconds on, 15 seconds off. Keep efforts and rest intervals regular, and build on these to progress. *Always take one full minute's rest between rounds.*			*See Session 1 for some ideas about how you might structure your rounds of punchbag work.*
• 3 x 3-minute rounds • 1 x minute's rest between rounds *Total 12 minutes* If necessary, split each round into manageable efforts: e.g. 60 seconds on, 15 seconds off. Keep efforts and rest intervals regular, and build on these to progress. *Always take one full minute's rest between rounds.*	Skipping *(skipping rope)*	66	For cardiovascular fitness; muscular endurance; speed, balance and co-ordination; psychological benefits (focus, discipline). Master the basic two-footed technique and/or "running in place." Then vary techniques and routines for progression. This is an impact activity: wear cushioned footwear and use a "giving" floor-surface.

Minutes/Rounds	Activity (equipment needed)	Page ref.	Comments
• 2 x 3-minute rounds • 1 x minute's rest *Total 8 minutes*	Focus pads (*hand-wraps beneath bag or sparring gloves*)	75	Addresses every aspect of boxing training – comprehensive boxing fitness workout. Perform only with a qualified instructor. *See Session 1 for some examples of the punches, combinations, footwork and defensive/evasive techniques your trainer may ask you to perform.*
6 minutes	Non-boxing cardio activity (*various; see Comments*)		Further improves cardiovascular fitness and muscular endurance; enhances recovery between rounds; speeds body fat reduction. Suitable activities include jogging and cycling; or gym machines such as stepper, cross-trainer, exercise bike, treadmill. Choose one activity per session, and vary from session to session if possible.
5 minutes	Core training (*mat or towel; other – e.g. Swiss ball, medicine ball*) **OR** Resistance training (*mat; other – e.g. dumbbells*) **OR** A combination of core and resistance training (*mat; other – varies*)	139 148	Core training strengthens abdominal and other core muscles. Improves posture, and has beneficial effect on boxing techniques. Resistance work strengthens specific muscles or muscle groups. Improves muscular endurance and encourages body fat reduction. Improves posture, and has beneficial effect on boxing techniques. You can perform your core and resistance exercises either in groups of *repetitions* (single efforts), or over set *intervals* (time periods). *See Session 1 for some examples of how you might structure your core/resistance work, but increase the workload to reflect your more advanced fitness level by performing the exercises for longer (duration), harder (intensity), and/or more often (frequency). More guidance on training variables can be found on page 150.*
5 minutes	Cool-down	35	Encourages the body to return gradually to its pre-exercise state. Perform gentle, static stretches for each part of the body. Remove wet clothing from next to the skin, and put on dry layers.

NB: Always take water to your session; sip little and often.

BOXING FITNESS SESSION 3: ADVANCED LEVEL

DURATION: 1 HOUR 40 MINUTES

This session assumes that you have access to the full range of personal equipment listed in PART TWO. Alternatives to some of the techniques are suggested in Session 5 on page 125.

Minutes/Rounds	Activity (equipment needed)	Page ref.	Comments
10 minutes	Wrap your hands (hand-wraps)	23	Do this before every boxing fitness session. Protects your hands inside boxing gloves; encourages a "professional" and focused attitude; and helps keep your hands in the correct position as you make a fist.
	Warm-up: "pulse-raiser"	35	Light cardiovascular exercise. Raises your heart rate; lubricates your joints; and increases the elasticity of your muscles. Suitable activities include jogging or cycling; or in the gym, treadmill, step, cross-trainer or exercise bike – choose one of these activities for your pulse-raiser, and try to vary your choice from session to session.
	Warm-up: dynamic stretches	41	Sport-specific movements designed to mobilize your joints and prepare your body for boxing training. Try those recommended on page 41, or research/design your own. Replicate boxing movements: e.g. rotational (hips, torso, shoulders, for punching), and squatting (stance and footwork).
• 6 x 3-minute rounds • 1 x minute's rest between rounds *Total 24 minutes*	Shadow boxing (hand-wraps)	64	For cardiovascular fitness; muscular endurance; technical rehearsal; speed, balance and co-ordination; psychological benefits (focus, discipline). Practice individual punches, combinations, defensive/evasive techniques, and footwork. Ideally perform all, or in part, in front of a mirror, to monitor form and provide a "shadow" opponent.

Minutes/Rounds	Activity (equipment needed)	Page ref.	Comments
If necessary, split each round into manageable efforts: e.g. 60 seconds on, 15 seconds off. Keep efforts and rest intervals regular, and build on these to progress. *Always take one full minute's rest between rounds.*			*See Session 1 for ideas on how you might structure your rounds of shadow boxing.*
• 6 x 3-minute rounds • 1 x minute's rest between rounds *Total 24 minutes* If necessary, split each round into manageable efforts: e.g. 60 seconds on, 15 seconds off. Keep efforts and rest intervals regular, and build on these to progress. *Always take one full minute's rest between rounds.*	Punching bag *(hand-wraps beneath bag or sparring gloves)*	70	Provides resistance to punches and encourages reflexive, mobile response. For cardiovascular fitness; muscular endurance; strength/power; speed; technical rehearsal; psychological benefits (including channeling aggression). Practice individual punches, combinations, defensive/evasive techniques, and footwork. *See Session 1 for ideas on how you might structure your rounds of bag work.*

Minutes/Rounds	Activity (equipment needed)	Page ref.	Comments
• 6 x 3-minute rounds • 1 x minute's rest between rounds *Total 24 minutes* If necessary, split each round into manageable efforts: e.g. 60 seconds on, 15 seconds off. Keep efforts and rest intervals regular, and build on these to progress. *Always take one full minute's rest between rounds.*	Skipping *(skipping rope)*	66	For cardiovascular fitness; muscular endurance; speed, balance and co-ordination; psychological benefits (focus, discipline). Master the basic two-footed technique and/or "running in place." Then vary techniques and routines for progression. This is an impact activity: wear cushioned footwear and use a "giving" floor-surface.
• 2 x 3-minute rounds • 1 x minute's rest *Total 8 minutes*	Focus pads *(hand-wraps beneath bag or sparring gloves)*	75	Addresses every aspect of boxing training – comprehensive boxing fitness workout. Perform only with a qualified instructor. *See Session 1 for some examples of the punches, combinations, footwork and defensive/evasive techniques your trainer may ask you to perform.*

Minutes/Rounds	Activity (equipment needed)	Page ref.	Comments
5 minutes	Core training (mat or towel; other – e.g. Swiss ball, medicine ball)	139	Core training strengthens abdominal and other core muscles. Improves posture, and has beneficial effect on boxing techniques.
	OR Resistance training (mat; other – e.g. dumbbells)	148	Resistance work strengthens specific muscles or muscle groups. Improves muscular endurance and encourages body fat reduction. Improves posture, and has beneficial effect on boxing techniques.
	OR A combination of core and resistance training (mat; other – varies)		You can perform your core and resistance exercises either in groups of *repetitions* (single efforts), or over set *intervals* (time periods). *See Session 1 for some examples of how you might structure your core/resistance work, but increase the workload to reflect your more advanced fitness level by performing the exercises for longer (duration), harder (intensity), and/or more often (frequency). More guidance on training variables can be found on page 150.*
5 minutes	Cool-down	35	Encourages the body to return gradually to its pre-exercise state. Perform gentle, static stretches for each part of the body. Remove wet clothing from next to the skin, and put on dry layers.

NB: Always take water to your session; sip little and often.

BOXING FITNESS SESSION 4: ADVANCED LEVEL – ALTERNATIVE/PROGRESSION

DURATION: 1 HOUR

This session assumes that you have access to the full range of personal equipment listed in *PART TWO*. Alternatives to some of the techniques are suggested in Session 5 on page 125.

Minutes	Activity (equipment needed)	Page ref.	Comments
10 minutes	Wrap hands (hand-wraps) Warm-up: "pulse-raiser" and dynamic stretches	23	Prepare and warm up exactly as for **BOXING FITNESS SESSION 3: ADVANCED LEVEL.**
6 minutes	Shadow boxing (hand-wraps)	64	Continuous effort with no rest. Pace yourself and include all the punches, combinations, defensive/evasive techniques, and footwork. Work hard – this should make you sweaty and breathless. *See Session 1 for ideas on how you might structure your shadow boxing – but perform those ideas continuously over the full 6 minutes without stopping.*
• 1 x minute continual punching, 10-second rest *Perform this × 6, followed by 1 x minute's recovery* • 1 x minute continual punching, 10-second rest *Perform this × 6, followed by 1 x minute's recovery* Total 14 minutes	Punching bag (hand-wraps under bag or sparring gloves)	70	Stand close to the bag with your guard up. Throw out a jab followed by a cross, and keep alternating these two shots without pause, to achieve a fluid punching motion. Remember to breathe! At the end of each minute, when you are taking your 10-second rest, shake out your arms, take some deep breaths, and begin again. *Tip:* When your arms begin to tire, try shifting the emphasis away from them to the rotational movement of your torso – i.e. making contact with the bag's surface by twisting your upper body, more than by pushing the punches out.

Minutes	Activity (equipment needed)	Page ref.	Comments
IF YOU HAVE A FOCUS PAD TRAINER, YOU CAN PERFORM THE FOLLOWING 15-MINUTE FOCUS PAD WORKOUT AS AN ALTERNATIVE TO THE PUNCHING BAG WORK SPECIFIED ABOVE.			
IF YOU ARE ABLE TO DO BOTH, ALTERNATE BETWEEN THE PUNCHING BAG WORK AND THE FOCUS PAD WORK, SESSION BY SESSION, FOR THE DURATION OF YOUR PROGRAM AT THIS LEVEL.			
• 1 x 15 minutes continuous, with no rest	Focus pads (hand-wraps beneath bag or sparring gloves)	75	Your trainer will call out punches, combinations and moves over a 15-minute period. They will know your fitness level and abilities, and will help you pace your work accordingly. *See Session 1 for some examples of the punches, combinations, footwork and defensive/evasive techniques your trainer may ask you to perform over this continuous 15-minute period.*
• 1 x minute continual skipping, 10-second rest *Perform this × 6, followed by 1 × minute's recovery* • 1 x minute continual skipping, 10-second rest *Perform this × 6, followed by 1 × minute's recovery* *Total 14 minutes*	Skipping (skipping rope)	66	Begin with the basic two-footed technique, and/or with running in place. As you progress, you can start to increase the pace at which you skip, and/or introduce a variety of more advanced techniques. (If you are very fit and skilled, try a full minute of double-unders!)

Minutes	Activity (equipment needed)	Page ref.	Comments
10 minutes	Core work and resistance work combined (various)	139 148	As for **BOXING FITNESS SESSION 3: ADVANCED LEVEL**, but progress by increasing the number, type or complexity of the core and resistance exercises. To be able to sustain high-intensity boxing training at this level, without compromising posture or technique, you need very good core fitness, muscle strength, and muscular endurance.
5 minutes	Cool-down	35	Encourages the body to return gradually to its pre-exercise state. Perform gentle, static stretches for each part of the body. Remove wet clothing from next to the skin, and put on dry layers.

NB: Always take water to your session; sip little and often.

BOXING FITNESS SESSION 5: WITH MINIMUM PERSONAL EQUIPMENT

DURATION: 1 HOUR

This session assumes that you have access only to hand-wraps, a skipping rope and a personal interval timer. Because of this, it can be performed anywhere – including outdoors, or at home.

Note: Make sure you have sufficient clear space to work in, with no potential slipping or tripping hazards.

Minutes/Rounds	Activity (equipment needed)	Page ref.	Comments
5 minutes	Wrap your hands (hand-wraps)	23	Protects your hands inside boxing gloves; encourages a "professional" and focused attitude; and helps keep your hands in the correct position as you make a fist.
10 minutes	Warm-up: 'pulse-raiser'	35	Light cardiovascular exercise. Suitable outdoor activities include jogging or cycling – choose one activity per session. At home, you can jog on the spot, or up and down the stairs – anything that serves to raise your heart rate; lubricate your joints; and increase the elasticity of your muscles.
	Warm-up: static stretches	37	Increases range of motion of joints; may decrease the likelihood of injury and post-session stiffness. Include at least one stretch for each of the following: neck, shoulders, chest, upper back, lower back, waist, front of thighs, back of thighs, calves, ankles. Enter into stretch gently, hold each stretch for 10-15 seconds, and do not bounce. Maintain good posture; add variety.
	Warm-up: dynamic stretches	41	Sport-specific movements designed to mobilize your joints and prepare your body for boxing training. Try those recommended on page 41, or research/design your own. Replicate boxing movements: e.g. rotational (hips, torso, shoulders, for punching), and squatting (stance and footwork).

Minutes/Rounds	Activity (equipment needed)	Page ref.	Comments
• 6 x 2-minute rounds • 30-second rest between rounds *Total 18 minutes*	Shadow boxing *(hand-wraps)*	64	Note that the rounds have decreased from 3 to 2 minutes, and the rest period from 1 minute to 30 seconds. This is because you will dedicate each round to a different punch or combination; a particular defensive/evasive move or series of movements; or a variety of footwork. Here is an example, but you can devise your own. (Use your imagination, keep it at a pace and complexity suitable to your fitness level, and remember to take a full 30-second rest between the rounds): • Round 1: 2 minutes of jabs and crosses (rehearse single jabs, double jabs, double-jab cross, one-two, one-two-three, four straight') • Round 2: 2 minutes of hooks and hook combinations (rehearse single hooks, double hooks, jab-hook-cross, jab-double hook-cross, double jab-hook-cross) • Round 3: 2 minutes as above, but with uppercuts and uppercut combinations • Round 4: 2 minutes rehearsing your footwork, with your guard up and no punches thrown (move in different directions, bounce "in and out" on your toes, circle an imaginary opponent, "roll" back and forward as if evading counterpunches) • Round 5: 2 minutes of evasive and defensive techniques (slipping, bobbing and weaving, and counterpunching in response to imagined shots from an opponent) • Round 6: *either* 1 minute of continual punching and footwork, with 10 seconds rest, and repeat; *or* 2 minutes combining all the techniques practiced in Rounds 1-5

Minutes/Rounds	Activity (equipment needed)	Page ref.	Comments
• 6 x 1-minute rounds • 30-second rest between rounds	Skipping (skipping rope)	66	Depending on your ability and fitness level, aim to increase the pace and complexity of each minute of skipping. For example: • Minute 1: basic two-footed technique, at a steady pace • Minute 2: using the same technique, pick up the pace until it's as fast as you're able to skip without burning yourself out or stumbling too often • Minute 3: running in place, at a steady pace • Minute 4: using the same technique, pick up the pace until it's as fast as you're able to skip without burning yourself out or stumbling too often • Minute 5: switch constantly between the two techniques • Minute 6: combining both techniques, move around as you skip – forward, backward, side to side, around an imaginary square, and so on As you progress, you can start to introduce a wider range of techniques. Try the ones described on page 67, or make up some of your own.

Minutes/Rounds	Activity (equipment needed)	Page ref.	Comments
DEPENDING ON WHETHER YOU ARE IN A GYM OR OUTDOOR ENVIRONMENT, OR AT HOME, FOLLOW SKIPPING WITH:			
8-10 minutes	Non-boxing cardio activity *(various; see Comments)*	n/a	**Outdoors:** via a safe and well-lit route, jog (or walk/jog, depending on your fitness level) for the given period. Vary the intensity of your efforts. For example: • 1 x minute brisk walk • 1 x minute slow jog • 1 x minute harder effort *Repeat 3 times* **In the gym:** perform 8-10 x minutes of step machine, treadmill, cross-trainer and/or exercise bike. Stay with one machine, or mix them up. As above, vary the intensity of your efforts. This is more effective in building stamina and reducing body fat. **Outdoors, in the gym, or at home:** another option is to perform an abbreviated version of the *boxing circuit*. See pages 129-136 for a detailed description.
5 minutes	Core training *(towel)* **OR** Bodyweight resistance training **OR** A combination of core and resistance training *(towel)*	139 148	Core training strengthens abdominal and other core muscles. Improves posture, and has beneficial effect on boxing techniques. Resistance work strengthens specific muscles or muscle groups. Improves muscular endurance and encourages body fat reduction. Improves posture, and has beneficial effect on boxing techniques. You can perform your core and resistance exercises either in groups of *repetitions* (single efforts), or over set *intervals* (time periods). Choose exercises that require no equipment – for example, you will use your own bodyweight for resistance work. See Session 1 for some ideas on how you might structure your core/resistance training.
3-5 minutes	Cool-down	35	Encourages the body to return gradually to its pre-exercise state. Perform gentle, static stretches for each part of the body. Remove wet clothing from next to the skin, and put on dry layers.

BOXING CIRCUIT

DURATION: UP TO 1 HOUR*

See page 107 of this section for an introduction to boxing circuit training.
The circuit is extremely flexible, needing no equipment and minimal space.
Use it as an alternative to/substitute for any of the boxing fitness techniques.
*Adapt the duration according to requirements.

The boxing circuit lends itself well to a class/group environment – try it with your partner, and/or some friends.

Exercise/activity	Number/minutes	Recovery	Comments
Warm-up: on-the-spot jogging followed by gentle static stretches	3–5 minutes	N/A	See page 37 for some recommended stretches, or devise your own. Hold each stretch for 10–15 seconds. Don't bounce.
Dynamic punching: while jogging on the spot, punching continually up above your head, out in front of you, out to your sides, circling your arms – anything you feel like, as long as your arms and legs are in constant motion	1 x 3-minute round	N/A	This is your "pulse-raiser." Make it active, and fun! If you need to stop jogging for a break, continue moving – try stepping briskly from side to side, swinging your arms.
Shadow boxing	3 x 3-minute rounds	1 x minute's rest between rounds	Practice individual punches, combinations, defensive/evasive techniques, and footwork. Ideally perform all, or part, of your shadow boxing in front of a mirror, to monitor form and provide a "shadow" opponent. *See Session 1 for some ideas of how to put together your rounds of shadow boxing.*

Exercise/activity	Number/minutes	Recovery	Comments
Move onto the circuit exercises, as follows:			
"Burpees"	10 reps	Perform 10 repetitions of each exercise, in the sequence given, with no rest between. Repeat this sequence twice more – again, with no rest (so you are doing 30 of each exercise in total). This should take you exactly 3 minutes (e.g. 1 full round).	**The technique for each exercise is described and illustrated below.**
Star jumps	10 reps		
Squat thrusts	10 reps		
Split-leg squat thrusts	10 reps		
Directional squat jumps	10 reps		
Straight/tuck jumps	10 reps		
		Take 1 x minute's rest	
		REPEAT THE ROUND AS ABOVE	
		Take 1 x minute's rest	
		REPEAT THE ROUND AS ABOVE, A THIRD AND FINAL TIME	
		Take 2 x minutes' rest	
"Burpees"	1 x minute continuous	Perform each exercise over the course of 1 x minute. Then take 1 x minute's rest between each exercise.	Depending on your fitness level, you may well not be able to perform any or all of the exercises for 1 x minute without stopping. This is OK! Simply keep going the best you can. Get into a rhythm and focus your mind.
Star jumps	1 x minute continuous		
Squat thrusts	1 x minute continuous		It can help to have a realistic goal to aim for: for example, perhaps experience has taught you that you can manage 20 "burpees" in the course of a minute. Aim for this each time you do the circuit, and see if you can beat your own best score.
Split-leg squat thrusts	1 x minute continuous		
Directional squat jumps	1 x minute continuous		
Straight/tuck jumps	1 x minute continuous		

Exercise/activity	Number/minutes	Recovery	Comments
		Take 2 x minutes rest	
Core and/or resistance training	5–10 minutes	N/A	See pages 142–157 for some recommended core/resistance training exercises, or research your own. *See Session 1 for some ideas on how you might structure your core/resistance work.*
Cool-down	5 minutes	N/A	Perform gentle static stretches, holding for 10–15 seconds each, for every part of the body as described on page 37.

*You can adapt the duration of the boxing circuit by:
(i) cutting down on the number of rounds
(ii) reducing the effort intervals (e.g. from 1 x minute to 1 x 30 seconds), and/or
(iii) reducing the recovery intervals.

Burpees

From standing, feet together and with good posture.

- Squat down and place your hands flat on the floor, one on either side of your knees.
- Shift your bodyweight over your hands and "jump" both feet backward, until you are in a push-up position.
- Jump your feet back to the squat position, between your arms.
- Stand back up, and repeat.
- The difficulty can be increased by adding a single vertical jump as you return to standing, before squatting back down to repeat the burpee.

Variation:

Start from standing as before, but with your legs slightly wider than hip-width apart. When you squat down, place your hands on the floor between your knees, instead of on either side of them. Jump your feet backward (still apart), and return them to the squat, one on either side of your hands. Stand back up, and repeat.

Star jumps

From standing, feet together and with good posture.

- Keeping your head up and chest lifted, bend your knees slightly. Your arms are down by your side.
- Jump into the air, simultaneously parting your legs and swinging your arms up toward the horizontal – so you are making a "star" position with your body.
- Before you land, bring your legs back together, and your arms back down to your sides.
- When you land, do so with some "give" in your knees, to minimize impact and to prepare for the next jump.

Variation:

When you jump, land on the floor with your legs apart and arms out to your sides – i.e. landing in the star position. Then jump your feet back together and lower your arms, before repeating.

Straight/tuck jumps

From standing.

- For this circuit exercise, you can either perform a tuck jump, for which your arms are held loosely by your side; or a straight jump, for which your arms are stretched above your head. The straight jump is slightly easier, so more suitable for the novice; it is also recommended for those with any lower-body joint problems, since it involves less impact with the floor.
- Initiate either jump by bending at the knees.
- For the tuck jump, when you leave the floor, draw your knees toward your chest so that your body achieves a tucked position. As you descend back toward the floor, your knees straighten out for the landing.
- For the straight jump, simply jump directly upward, keeping your knees straight and without lowering your arms. It's more like a bounce than a jump.
- Repeat the jumps over the required time, or for the required number of repetitions. For the one-minute section of the circuit, you could add variety by alternating the two types of jump – e.g. 10 straight jumps, 10 tuck jumps, repeat.

Squat thrusts

From a squat position, with your feet between your hands.

- The squat thrust is essentially a burpee (page 132), without the standing-up part.
- As for the burpee, jump your feet backwards until you are in a push-up position.
- Then jump them straight back to the squat position, between your arms.
- Do not stand up, but simply repeat this "in-out" movement with your legs for the desired time or number of times.
- If you have limited mobility, and find it difficult to perform the squat thrust over the whole range as illustrated, simply reduce the distance over which you "jump" your feet – effectively performing a half squat-thrust.

Split-leg squat thrusts

From a squat position, with your left knee bent and right foot between your hands, and your right leg stretched behind you as illustrated, toes "tucked under" and weight on the ball of the foot. The position is a little like a "sprint start."

- Perform the exercise as for a squat thrust (above), but with your legs split.
- Pushing off both feet simultaneously, "jump" your right leg forward and your left leg backward, so that you are basically achieving the start position but with your legs the other way around.
- Immediately repeat, so that you are switching your legs in an ongoing motion for the desired time or number of repetitions.
- If you have limited mobility and find it hard to perform the exercise over the whole range as illustrated, simply reduce the distance over which you "jump" your legs, so that your feet are closer together (i.e. the split is a little less wide).

Directional squat jumps

From standing, with your knees slightly bent and your arms crossed over your chest.

- Make sure you do not bend your back or "drop" your head and chest. Keep a "neutral spine" – see page 36. Your whole body should be angled, so that instead of facing directly forward, you are standing at 45 degrees to the right as illustrated.
- By pushing off both feet and straightening at the knees, initiate a small jump into the air, landing with bent knees in a shallow squat.
- The jump is not directly upward; you are aiming to turn your body in the air, so that you finish at an angle of 45 degrees in the opposite direction. Imagine the face of a clock: your start position was 10 minutes to 12; when you land, your body is now positioned at 10 past 12.
- Repeat the directional squat jump, returning to your start position. Perform the exercise for the required time or number of repetitions.
- Take the squat only as deep as is comfortable; there should be no undue strain on your knee joints. The knees should never extend past the toes.

In this final part of the book, we discuss three training elements which can greatly enhance your boxing fitness program, despite the fact that they don't directly involve boxing techniques. These are:

- Core (abdominal) training
- Resistance (weight) training
- Running ("roadwork")

Keep an open mind, and read on! Even if you are someone who "really hates running" or "never lifts weights," there are many different ways to incorporate these types of training into your boxing sessions – and significant benefits to be gained from them, no matter what your ability level or fitness goals.

In these chapters we certainly don't recommend that you set the alarm for 4.30 a.m. and pound the pavement, or lift heavy weights, or do hundreds of abdominal crunches: none of this is necessary. Just try integrating a few of our suggestions into your program, and see how they suit you. If you find them beneficial, you can build the techniques up gradually. If you really don't like them, omit them or substitute one type of training for another. It's a process of trial and error – in the end you will find the best combination for you.

Core training

In recent years, there has been increased recognition of the important role played by *core fitness* – also known as *core strength*, or *core stability* – both in sporting performance, and in contributing to our overall daily health and well-being. It is particularly important for the part it plays in reducing or preventing back pain.

In this chapter, we look at what the "core" consists of, and explore the particular benefits that good core strength can bestow. Finally we suggest some ways in which you can include core training in your boxing fitness program, to help progress your personal goals.

The core consists of the muscles in your abdomen, sides and spine

>> Defining the core

The core can be defined *as all the muscles that stabilize, align and move the trunk of the body*. It can actually help to think of it in terms of an apple core: this runs through the fruit from top to bottom, forming a sturdy cylinder around which the edible part grows.

The human core is somewhat similar, in that it is composed of everything that maintains the upright posture of the body: namely, the abdominal muscles; the muscles in your sides (the *obliques*); and the muscles between the vertebrae in your spine, which keep it in alignment.

Considering it like this ensures that we take account not only of the surface core muscles – such as the *rectus abdominus*, otherwise known as the elusive "six-pack" – but also the deeper internal muscles, all of which help us to maintain stability in motion.

Boxers need good core strength to cope with repeated blows to their body, and to maintain a solid, balanced stance throughout contests which may last as long as 12 rounds. Old-school trainers often drop weighted medicine balls onto their fighters' stomachs, to give them both the physical and mental ability to cope with body shots. Don't try it at home ... or anywhere else!

back and your belly pulled in. Whether you work at a desk all day, or are on your feet for long periods of time, you will feel less tired if you have a strong core to support you. As a result, stress and strain are less likely to build up in vulnerable areas of your body, such as your neck, shoulders and back.

All of this can make an enormous difference not only to how you look, but also to how you feel. If your body is well aligned and relaxed, you will be comfortable in it. If you are comfortable in your body, your body language will be positive – which has a domino effect on how others view and respond to you.

>> The benefits of a strong core

In terms of your boxing fitness sessions, the stronger your core, the better you will be able to perform the various techniques correctly – thus getting the most out of your training, while significantly reducing the likelihood of stiffness or injury.

More generally, good core stability will improve your posture and appearance, so that you naturally hold yourself "taller," with your shoulders down and

>> Fast, measurable results

One of the beauties of core training is that it works quickly, and this is very motivating. If, say, you were to try a "front plank" (described below) for the first time, you might be able to hold the position for 10–20 seconds at best. But if you were then to practice the exercise once a day in front of the TV, in a couple of weeks you would be able to sustain it for much longer. After a while, you would start to notice the beneficial effects of core training while performing everyday activities such as lifting a heavy object or placing something on a high shelf.

Keep a record

Core exercises usually consist of either a held position, such as a plank; or a movement that you repeat a given number of times (known as *repetitions*) or over a particular time period.

> I started boxing training because I thought I needed to lose a lot of weight. I'm taller and bustier than my friends, and for ages I just felt heavy and self-conscious. My boxing instructor set me a program of cardio punching and core training, and after a few weeks I really started noticing a difference. Some weight had come off, it's true – but I was surprised to realize that most of the improvement was in my posture. I don't "stoop" any more, and I'm quite proud of my body when I catch sight of myself in the mirror!
>
> Maggie, 20
> Student

This is a good example of where keeping a *training diary* (see pages 104–106) really helps. You may set yourself targets – if you are training solo – or your instructor may set them for you, session by session. Depending on which exercise(s) you are working on that day, you can record your results in the following ways:

- A *repetition* is a single, complete effort/exercise that may be repeated any number of times.

- A *set* is a group of repetitions performed continuously without stopping, usually followed by a specific period of rest (*recovery*).

> For a held position, note down the time for which you were able to perform the exercise *while maintaining good technique* (if your technique starts to suffer, relax the pose; continuing after this point is counter-productive and may even lead to injury).

> For an exercise you have to repeat a given number of times (known as a *set*), jot down whether or not you were able to complete the task – and if you weren't, the number you reached before you stopped. You can aim to beat this next time around.

> For an exercise you are to perform over a given time period (e.g. the number of abdominal crunches you can do in 30 seconds, always with good technique), write down how many you achieved; this is your "personal best," and you can build on it as you work through your program.

If you keep an accurate record of your efforts and achievements, after a relatively short period of time your diary will reveal dramatic improvements in your core fitness. This is a great feeling – one which in itself can have you holding your head up higher, and your back and shoulders straighter.

Be sure to keep up the good work, because soon you will see direct evidence of it in your boxing techniques. Remember, the core consists of *all the muscles that stabilize, align and move your upper body*. So if your core is solid, your stance will feel more grounded and sustainable; your punches will have more power, because they are generated from a position of stability and strength; and your

footwork and skipping will be more balanced. It's a win-win situation: don't skip your core work.

>> Core training equipment

The only equipment you need for basic core training is a reasonably cushioned exercise mat. However, if you are able to purchase (and have room to store) a Swiss ball, this can be a real bonus. See the illustrations on pages 146–47 for an example of a Swiss ball.

Information on the original Swiss ball can be found at www.swissballs.com, but many varieties now exist and may be known by different names, including gym ball, exercise ball and stability ball. The primary benefit of using one of these balls for your core training, rather than a hard, flat surface, is the introduction of the element of *instability*.

In order to counter the ball's instability, and thus balance itself to perform a particular exercise, your body has to engage many more muscles than it would on a stable surface – and the primary muscles used are those which make up your core (the abdominals, the obliques, and the muscles of the back). Because this makes Swiss ball exercises so effective in isolating those harder-to-reach parts of the core, such as the lower abdominals, we have included one or two of them in this chapter, and would encourage you to consider investing in an exercise ball for your boxing fitness program.

You can buy a Swiss ball from most sports outlets, and many department stores now stock them too. The ball is basically a large inflatable sphere made of soft PVC and filled with air. It usually comes flat-packed with a foot pump, and is available in a range of sizes – the most common being 55 cm, 65 cm and 75 cm in diameter. The taller you are, the larger the ball you need; check the packaging, which will tell you the appropriate choice.

(You can further test the ball's suitability by sitting on it, in its inflated state. Your feet should be planted firmly on the floor, with your knees bent at right-angles. If the angle at your knees is greater than 90 degrees, you need a smaller ball; less than 90 degrees and you need a larger size.)

Follow the instructions to inflate the ball: when it's fully pumped up, the surface should give by only a couple of inches if you press down on it. Over time, it is inevitable that the ball will lose some air. It is important to keep it well-inflated, because if it becomes too soft, this may affect your technique. Balancing on the ball will also become easier, thus compromising your core fitness gains.

Don't worry if getting into position on your Swiss ball feels awkward initially, causing you to fumble around – or even fall off! This is normal, and you will soon become accustomed to it. You can have complete faith in the robustness of the ball: we've been using them for years, and haven't managed to burst one yet.

>> Some core training exercises

There is a huge range of core exercises and techniques that you can try, and it is not within the scope of this book to cover more than just a few. We recommend that you research your own, to find the ones that work best for you, and incorporate a variety into each of your boxing fitness sessions (preferably at the end, before the cool-down).

For each of the exercises listed below, we describe one full repetition. This may be repeated any number of times, and/or grouped in sets, according to what is specified in your program.

Basic abdominal curl (sit-up or crunch)

1 Lie on your back, with your feet on the floor and your knees bent. Your hands should be flat on the floor by your sides, palms down.

2 Contract (pull in) all your core muscles, simultaneously lifting your head and shoulders from the floor. As you do so, your hands slide along the floor in the direction of your feet – but only by a couple of inches; the crunch is a small movement, which is why the term "sit-up" is misleading.

3 Hold the "crunched" position as illustrated for 1–2 seconds, then relax and slowly lower your head and shoulders back to the floor.

Long lever abdominal crunch

This is a progression on the basic abdominal crunch described above.

1 Lie on your back, with your feet on the floor and your knees bent. Your arms are stretched out behind your head, with the elbows held close to the ears.

2 Contract (pull in) all your core muscles, simultaneously lifting your arms, head and shoulders from the floor *as one unit*. It is very important to keep your arms fixed, with the elbows held in close to your ears, as you lift up. This provides the "long lever" of the exercise's name, which increases its difficulty.

3 Hold the "crunched" position for 1–2 seconds, then relax and slowly lower your arms, head and shoulders back to the floor – once again as a unit.

Vertical leg abdominal crunch

This is another variant on the basic abdominal crunch, and represents a further progression from the "long lever" version described above.

1 Lie on your back with your legs raised, toes pointing up to the ceiling. Your knees should be together and slightly bent. Your hands are beside your ears.

2 Contract (pull in) all your core muscles, simultaneously lifting your head and shoulders slightly off the floor.

3 From this position, further pull in your core muscles and move your torso toward your legs. It's important that you keep your legs still: don't be tempted to "cheat" by moving them toward your torso, rather than the other way around!

4 Hold the lifted position for 1–2 seconds before relaxing and slowly lowering your upper body back to the floor.

Note: When doing abdominal exercises, it is not advisable to hook your feet under anything – or to have a training partner or instructor hold them. This is because as soon as you do so, your *hip flexors* (the muscles at the top of your thighs, which act to bring the knee upwards) perform a large part of the work, taking the emphasis off the "abs."

Bicycle abdominal exercise

This exercise is very effective, but a little tricky – it requires focus and co-ordination to complete. If you find it difficult at first, persevere; even by trying, you will be gaining core fitness benefits.

1 Lie flat on the floor on your back, with your hands by your ears. Lift your feet off the mat and bring your knees toward your chest until they are at about a 45-degree angle.

2 Start to slowly perform a bicycle pedaling action – as if you were riding a bike while lying on your back!

3 Once you have this mastered, continuing the pedaling motion, contract your core muscles and raise your head and shoulders from the floor. As your left knee is coming toward you, attempt to touch your right elbow to it.

4 Keep pedaling, so that now your right knee starts to move toward you. Your upper body then twists slightly so that the left elbow is touched to the right knee.

5 Continue to alternate left elbow to right knee, right elbow to left knee, until you have achieved the desired number of repetitions. Then slowly relax your upper body and your legs back to the floor.

Back extensions

If you do a lot of work on your abdominal muscles, you must be careful to balance this with some back-strengthening exercises, so that the whole core is trained. Back extensions are a good way of doing this, and there are many variations on the basic exercise – some of which we describe below.

1 Lie on the floor on your front, with your arms down by your sides, looking straight ahead.

2 By pushing your stomach into the floor and simultaneously contracting all your core muscles, you should be able to lift your head and shoulders from the mat. The movement is a small one – that's fine.

3 Hold the extended position for 1–2 seconds, then relax and slowly lower your head and shoulders back to the floor.

Variations:

- Place your hands by your ears, instead of by your sides, and perform the back extension as described.
- Stretch your arms out horizontally and perform the back extension as described.
- Place your hands in the small of your back, and perform the back extension as described.
- Stretch your arms out in front of you, elbows by your ears, and perform the back extension as described. This one is harder work! To get the maximum benefit, make sure you keep your elbows next to your ears throughout, so that your head, arms and shoulders all raise up as one unit.
- Try the basic exercise as described, and any or all of the variations, while lifting your legs from the floor at the same time as you raise your head and shoulders. If you can do this quite easily, attempt to initiate a rocking movement – so that your body replicates the movement of a rocking horse's "legs."

Front plank

1 Lie on your front on the mat, with your elbows beneath your shoulders, hands clasped together and forearms resting on the floor beneath your chest. Your toes should be tucked under. (It is acceptable to have your legs slightly apart, if you find this position more stable and comfortable when performing the exercise.)

2 Raise your body from the floor, so that the only contact with the mat is made by your feet and forearms. It is important that your body makes a flat, straight line, with your buttocks neither sticking up toward the ceiling nor sinking down towards the floor, causing your lower back to hollow.

3 Pull in all your core muscles and hold the plank position for as long as you can, before relaxing (under control!) back to the floor. As you continue to hold your body up, it may start to shake; this is a good training effect. But if your technique starts to suffer – with your lower back arching, for example – take a rest before resuming the plank, as many times as is specified for your session.

4 If you are feeling confident, try a progression on the basic front plank. Achieve a solid plank position as described above, then attempt to lift one leg from the ground for a few seconds. Make sure that you don't do this by twisting your pelvis: keep both hips level, parallel to the ground. Lower the leg and repeat on the other side.

Side plank

This is a variation on the basic front plank: make sure you attempt it on both sides! Your ultimate aim could be to move from a side plank, over to a front plank, and over once more to a plank on the other side – holding each position for a set amount of time, without letting your body relax on to the mat at anytime.

1 For a left-sided plank as illustrated, lie on your left side on the mat, with your left elbow under your shoulder and the forearm and hand resting on the floor.

2 Your legs should be straight and slightly parted, with your right leg over the top and in front of the left.

3 Raise your left hip from the floor until your body makes a straight line, with your weight supported on the forearm and feet. Check your alignment: your hips should not be rotated – either up toward the ceiling, or down towards the floor. Your buttocks should be tucked in. You can place your right arm on your right hip, or stretch it up towards the ceiling if you prefer.

4 Hold the side plank position for as long as possible, or until your technique begins to waver. Lower your body slowly back to the mat, turn over, and repeat on the other side.

Swiss ball abdominal crunch

1 Maneuver yourself onto the Swiss ball until you are lying on it as illustrated, with the ball underneath your back and your legs, bent at the knee, supporting you. Place your hands by your ears. It may take a little while to learn how to "lie down" on the ball. It's a process of trial and error!

2 With your feet planted firmly on the floor, lift your pelvis (which, if you are in the correct position, should be clear of the ball, not resting on it) so that the front of your body makes a flat plane.

3 Contract (pull in) your core muscles, at the same time lifting your head and shoulders from the ball. Hold the position for 1–2 seconds, then relax and lower your head and shoulders slowly back to the start position.

Never link your hands behind your head when doing abdominal exercises, as this can lead you inadvertently to pull on and perhaps strain your neck.

Swiss ball abdominal roll

This exercise, and the one that follows, are great for isolating and strengthening the lower abdominals.

1 Kneel on the mat with the Swiss ball in front of you. Place your hands palm-down on the top of the ball, with your arms straight and parallel.

2 Contract your core muscles and slowly roll the ball forward, keeping your arms as straight as possible. Your whole body should tilt forward when rolling the ball as illustrated: it helps to think about keeping your back flat, so that it does not arch or hollow.

3 When you have rolled the ball as far as possible, and before your technique starts to suffer (or you collapse!), press down on the ball with your hands, simultaneously pulling it back toward your body. Keep your arms as straight as possible, and focus on squeezing the abdominal muscles to move the ball back toward the start position.

Swiss ball abdominal pike

1 Maneuever yourself into position so that you are lying on the Swiss ball as illustrated, with the ball beneath your hips and upper thighs. Your hands are placed flat on the floor in front of you, beneath your shoulders. Your legs should be held together and be pointing straight out behind you.

2 Contract your core muscles, and, keeping your legs straight, think about pushing your buttocks up toward the ceiling. If you focus on strongly pulling in your lower abdominal muscles, your body should start to "pike" in the middle. As it does, the Swiss ball will begin to roll along your legs toward your feet.

3 Take the movement as far as you can while remaining securely in position on the Swiss ball. You may only move the ball a couple of inches when you first try this exercise – that's fine. You can build on your achievement over time, as your core strength improves.

4 Hold the piked position for 1–2 seconds, then slowly lower your buttocks and allow the ball to roll back to the start position.

16 Resistance training

>> What is resistance training?

In one form or another, all boxers use resistance work to enhance their training and optimize their performance in the ring. The main benefits to a fighter (and therefore to you) are increased muscle strength and size, and improved body composition. Resistance training also enhances muscular endurance, posture and range of motion – all of which, as we have seen, are required by a competitive boxer.

Until relatively recently, it was more common to refer to "weight training" than to "resistance training," but the old terminology is misleading. You don't need to lift weights to undertake a resistance-based workout; in fact, you can do a highly effective session using just the weight of your own body. This is good news for you, because it means that even if you can't get to a gym, you are still able to incorporate resistance work into your boxing fitness program.

The principle behind resistance training is the same as for any type of fitness training – one of *overload and adaptation*. Put simply, this means working the body harder than it normally would ("overloading" it), in order to induce a particular improvement in fitness (the "adaptation"). The body adapts to the increased workload to become more efficient – so that it can perform the same task with less effort next time around.

Resistance training will make you stronger, but it will not turn you into the Incredible Hulk! You can build muscle bulk with a type of weight training known as *hypertrophy* – but this requires a particular combination of effort, diet and recovery. The type of resistance work we cover here will not increase the size of your muscles to any significant degree.

Note that positive adaptations do not take place during the effort/overload phase (your training sessions), but rather in the recovery period that follows. For this reason it is very important to rest between your training sessions, if you are to see the full benefit of all your hard work. How much recovery you need depends on many factors, and so is difficult to define – but in Part Two we recommend that you leave at least 48 hours between your boxing fitness sessions, and this is a good guide to follow.

With resistance training, you overload your muscles by making them work against an opposing force. That force *resists* the effort you are making (hence the name), and is usually – but not always – gravity. When you perform a simple dumbbell squat as described below, you are working against gravity as it pulls the combined weight of your body and the dumbbells toward the floor.

Another good examples of resistance work is swimming – particularly against a tide or current, or in an exercise pool where a jet of water simulates a strong current.

>> The benefits

Regular resistance work, of a type and level that is appropriate to your personal training goals, can greatly progress your boxing fitness. Some of the benefits will be visible, such as improvements in your *body composition* (see page 14); others may be less visible but are no less important – for example, enhanced muscular endurance, and increased bone density and strength.

> Many people are surprised to learn that weight training leads to weight *loss*, but resistance work is a very effective way of encouraging body fat reduction. It raises your *metabolic rate* (the amount of energy you expend in a given period of time) so that you burn more calories for longer.

In terms of your boxing techniques, resistance work will enable you to punch harder and more often, and to sustain your efforts over a longer period of time. You can train your muscles to achieve any or all of these fitness gains, by altering what we refer to collectively as the *training variables*. These are:

> **Duration**: refers to the time period over which you perform an exercise. To increase duration, simply train for longer. For example, you could do bodyweight squats over 30-second intervals, and then progress gradually to one-minute intervals.

> **Intensity**: refers to how hard you are working in an exercise. To increase intensity, raise your effort level. For example, you might do a set of bodyweight squats, and then a further set with the added resistance of a pair of dumbbells.

> **Frequency**: refers to how often you perform an exercise. To increase frequency, do the exercise more frequently. For example, you could progress from two sets of 12 squats to three sets of 12 squats.

"Playing" with these training variables will encourage your muscles to adapt to different types of increased workload – thus giving you the potential to box better, harder and faster than before.

> **"**
>
> I know guys are supposed to be into weight training and looking "buff," but I've always found it boring and skipped or rushed it at the gym. When I started boxing training, the coach advocated light free-weight resistance work to improve my punching speed, endurance and co-ordination. We soon discovered that my left arm is stronger than my right, even though my stance is orthodox, and are gradually correcting this via a lot of dumbbell exercises. It's more of a challenge now, and I'm seeing improvements in my boxing techniques.
>
> John, 29
> Office worker **"**

It is important to note that such positive adaptations will not last unless the higher effort levels are sustained. Furthermore, in order to see continued progression, you need to constantly raise those effort levels. So if you decide to undertake resistance training to enhance your boxing fitness, you need to keep it up. This is known as the "use it or lose it" principle, and must be factored into your program.

>> "Compound" versus "isolation" exercises

A quick note here on these two types of resistance exercise. A *compound* exercise is one that involves more than one joint, and thus works several muscles or muscle groups at the same time. A good example is the squat (see page 152), which uses the ankles, knees and hips, and engages many muscles in the lower body and core.

By contrast, an *isolation* exercise involves only one joint, and works one muscle or muscle group. An example is the biceps curl (see page 156), which uses only the elbows, and engages the biceps muscle at the front of your upper arm.

This is relevant to your boxing fitness, because resistance work is likely to form only a small part of your overall program. You therefore want to get the maximum benefit from just a few exercises. Compound exercises use more muscle groups, and so burn more calories; they give you a full-body workout faster, and improve your strength, co-ordination, stability and balance.

As a general rule, then, it is preferable to select this type of resistance work, to get the best possible results from your training. Whatever exercises you decide on, try to include at least one for every major part of the body: the lower body; the chest; the back; and the shoulders.

>> **Resistance training equipment**

Rubber-coated dumbbells are easy to come by

For the exercises we have selected, the maximum equipment you will need is a pair of light dumbbells (perhaps 3–4 kg for ladies, and 5–6 kg for men); a bench, step or chair; and a solid wall. If you have access to a gym or health club which is well-stocked with resistance machines and free weights, this is good, since it provides more potential for variety in your program.

If you are able to, it is worth purchasing some dumbbells for home and outdoor use. They are versatile and easy to store, and can help you keep track of your training progression in a measurable way. For example, your journal may show that last month, you could do 3 x 12 shoulder presses, with a 30-second recovery between sets, using 3 kg dumbbells. This month you did the same – but with 4 kg dumbbells. There it is, in black and white: you are stronger than you were.

Dumbbells are widely available from sports shops and department stores, and over the Internet – in fact, some of the larger supermarket chains now stock them too. They do not have to cost the earth: the pretty chrome ones are expensive, but you can buy much cheaper rubber-coated or plastic versions.

If you don't want to purchase any free weights at all for your boxing fitness sessions, you can always use ordinary household items to provide a resistance for your muscles to work against. Try bottles of water or cans of beans – be creative.

INSIDER INFO

Remember: it can be very useful to practice your resistance exercises in front of a mirror – especially if you are training on your own, without an instructor or partner. By keeping an eye on your posture and technique, you may be able to identify and correct minor problems or imbalances, without the need for external feedback.

Basic bodyweight squat

A compound exercise for your core and lower body.

1 Stand with good posture, feet hip-width apart and with your hands either folded across your chest or held up near your ears.

2 Initiate the squat by bending your knees and "sitting" down. The movement is a vertical one: your body lowers towards the floor with a straight back, and head and chest lifted to maintain a "neutral spine."

3 Take the squat to a depth at which you are comfortable. You should not feel any undue strain in your knees, and your heels should remain on the floor. Hold the squat position for 1–2 seconds, then straighten your knees to return to the start position.

Note: When performing any squatting movement, it is essential to maintain what is known as a *neutral spine*. This refers to the natural curvature made by your backbone, which – if correctly aligned – forms a gentle "S" shape when viewed from the side. Keeping a neutral spine minimizes any stress to your lower back, while ensuring that you are working the correct muscles.

Variations:

> The dumbbell squat (illustrated). This exercise is performed with the same technique as the basic bodyweight squat described above – the only difference is that you have a dumbbell in each hand. Hold the weights down by your sides with your arms relaxed.

> The Swiss ball squat, which is especially suitable for people suffering from minor back problems. Stand facing away from a solid wall, with the Swiss ball positioned in the small of your back (shuffle your feet out from the wall slightly, and lean back into the ball). Perform the squat in exactly the same way as the basic version; the ball will naturally "roll" up your spine as you do so, providing good support through the exercise.

Split squat

A compound exercise for your core and lower body.

1 This exercise can be performed with or without dumbbells. Start with good posture, feet hip-width apart, chin up and chest lifted.

2 Take a good step forward with one leg. Be sure to keep a hip-width distance between your feet as you step, to avoid "walking a tightrope" (stepping one foot directly in front of the other) and thus compromising your stability in the exercise. Both legs are slightly bent, with your front foot flat on the floor and the heel of your back foot raised.

3 In this split-legged position, perform a squat. It is important to make the squat a vertical, downward movement, with no "forward traveling" over the front knee. Throughout the exercise, keep your head and chest lifted. Hold the squat position for 1–2 seconds before returning to the start position. Repeat either a set number of times on one side and then on the other, or alternate between the two sides.

Variation:

> Forward lunge. This exercise can be performed with or without dumbbells. It is carried out exactly as for the split squat described above, except that instead of repeatedly squatting in place in the split-legged position, you push off from your front foot after one lunge and return the foot to the start position. Repeat a set number of times on one foot before changing to the other, or alternate between the two sides.

Duck squat

A compound exercise for your core and lower body, with special emphasis on the inner thighs.

1 This exercise can be performed with or without dumbbells. Start as you would for the basic squat, except that your feet, instead of facing forward, are turned out at around a 45-degree angle – like a ballet dancer. If you are using dumbbells, these are held against the front of your thighs, palms facing inward.

2 Keeping your head up and chest lifted, squat down. You will feel that the emphasis of this exercise is on your inner thighs. Hold the squat position for 1–2 seconds, before returning to the start position.

Side lunge

A compound exercise for your core and lower body.

1 This exercise can be performed with or without dumbbells. If you are using dumbbells, these are held against your upper thighs, palms facing inward. Start in the same position as you would for a basic bodyweight squat, with good posture.

2 Take a big step to one side. The lunging leg bends at the knee, with the other leg remaining straight. Both feet are flat on the floor, with the toes pointing forward. Look ahead, not down; keep your head and chest lifted throughout the exercise. If you are using dumbbells, these will naturally move as you lunge, one to each side of the lunging leg.

3 Return to the start position by pushing off the lunging leg and reversing the sideways step. You can either repeat the exercise a set number of times on one side, before changing to the other, or alternate between the two sides.

Shoulder press

A compound exercise for your shoulders and upper back.

1 This exercise can be performed sitting on a bench or chair, or standing. If you choose to stand, ensure that you keep a good strong core, to avoid arching and thus placing stress on your lower back. Use light dumbbells to provide the resistance, or household items such as bags of sugar or cans of beans.

2 Start with your hands up in a "don't shoot!" position. Your upper arms are parallel to the floor, with a right angle at the elbows so your forearms are pointing straight up to the ceiling. Keep your wrists strong.

3 Push your hands up toward the ceiling, extending your arms straight up above your head. Your hands bring the weights together, under control, at the top of the exercise. Don't let your shoulders bunch up with the effort; it can help to think about keeping a long neck throughout.

4 To return to the start position, bend your arms at the elbows and lower the weights slowly.

Push-up

A compound exercise for your upper body, especially the chest and upper arms.

1 Take the plank position with your hands shoulder-width apart and your elbows straight.

2 Bend your elbows, keeping them close to your sides, and lower your body towards the floor. Keep your back straight and try to ensure a straight line running from the back of your head to your heels at all times.

3 Before you reach the floor, straighten your arms again. The whole movement should be performed in a controlled fashion.

Variation:

> Wall push-ups. Stand facing a solid wall, with your feet about 18 inches away from it. Place your hands against the wall at chest level and, bending only at the elbows and taking your weight on your arms, tip your whole body towards the wall. Ensure that your back is straight, without arching or hollowing; it should remain in alignment throughout the movement. Then push away and straighten your arms to return to the start position.

Triceps dip

A compound exercise for your chest, shoulders and upper arms.

1 You can perform this exercise on a bench or chair, or on the floor; we describe the former version here. Start by sitting on the edge of the bench or chair, with your hands on the seat close to your buttocks. Your feet are flat on the floor. Keep your knees bent slightly if performing the basic triceps dip, or straighten them for an advanced version of the exercise.

2 Shift forward until your buttocks are clear of the chair and your weight is supported on your hands. Then bend your arms and dip your body down toward the floor.

3 Go down only as far as you feel comfortable; you must be confident that you can push your body back up again by squeezing the triceps muscles in the back of your upper arms. Repeat the dipping movement for the desired number of repetitions, only sitting back on to the chair at the end of the set.

4 A progression on the bent-legged triceps dip is to perform the exercise with straight legs (as illustrated). This is done exactly as above, except that your heels rest on the floor rather than your whole foot.

Biceps curl

An isolation exercise for the front of your upper arms.

1 Perform this exercise using dumbbells or any appropriate weight or household item that will provide a suitable resistance. Start standing, with good posture. Your arms are held straight down, close into your body with your hands (palms facing outward) against your upper thighs.

2 Keeping your elbows still and tucked tightly into your body, lift the weights slowly to just above the horizontal. In the gym, you may see people swinging their dumbbells up and down, from the thighs right up to the shoulders and back down; this compromises the impact of the exercise by bringing the element of momentum into play – it's cheating, in effect! – taking the emphasis away from the biceps muscles.

3 Slowly straighten your arms to return the weights to the start position, again keeping your elbows still and close to your body.

4 For a variant on this exercise, perform the curl with one arm only for the given number of repetitions, before changing to the other side; or alternate between the two sides. For one-handed biceps curls, make sure that you keep a strong core and don't shift the opposite hip outward to compensate – check your alignment in a mirror if possible.

Calf raise

An isolation exercise for the calf muscles in your lower legs.

1 This exercise can be done on the edge of a step, a wooden block, or any other suitable, raised surface. Both legs can be worked at the same time to start with; as you get stronger you can do the raises one leg at a time – holding a weight of some kind for further progression.

2 Stand on the balls of your feet only. You may need to touch the wall or another support to keep your balance.

3 Keeping your legs straight, and only flexing your ankle joints, lower the heels toward the floor until you feel a strong stretch in your calf muscles.

4 Then reverse the direction, without bouncing, and stretch up on your toes as far as you can. Lower your heels slowly back to the start position.

Variation:

You can perform this exercise balanced on the edge of a step, which provides a greater range of movement. You will really feel the stretch as you lower your heels below the level of the balls of your feet.

17 Running

INSIDER INFO

Boxers run to increase their stamina, which facilitates their recovery between rounds of sparring and competition. Sprints, hill running and interval training also improve speed, strength and power in the ring. But "roadwork" is as much about mental preparation as it is about physical fitness: Rocky's iconic run up the steps in Philadelphia was a victory of mind over body – the underdog rising to the challenge.

Unless you are an endurance athlete, or naturally suited to endurance-based activities, it may well be daunting to consider running as part of your boxing fitness program. For many of us, jogging is inevitably associated with fatigue, aching muscles and breathlessness – none of which is particularly pleasant on a Sunday morning that could be spent reading the paper over a latte and a croissant.

It can help to remember that boxers and other athletes probably feel the same. By all accounts they don't look forward to setting the alarm for an ungodly hour, and starting the day with a lonely five-mile jog. It must be especially hard, during the winter months, to pound the pavement in the dark and the cold.

But it is widely accepted that running confers fitness gains that are especially suited to the demands placed on a fighter by their chosen sport. No matter how many rounds of punching bag work, focus pads and sparring a boxer may complete in the gym, the fact remains that to be thoroughly prepared for the rigours of a competitive bout, they have to run.

You are doing a great job of following in a boxer's footsteps so far; running in them now represents the final part of your journey.

>> Two types of running

The science of running is very complex, and it is not within the scope of this book to address the subject in any detail. Instead we will touch briefly on two main types of "roadwork" – *steady running* and *interval running*. Boxers incorporate both into their routine, for different training effects.

1. Steady running

A continuous, steady run will improve the working capacity of your heart and lungs, together with their ability to deliver oxygen to your muscles. This enables you to recover more quickly between intense bursts of activity – which is exactly what a round of boxing training constitutes.

2. Interval running

This involves running relatively hard for a specified amount of time, following by a defined rest period, after which you repeat the hard effort – with the cycle continuing however many times (or for however long) your program dictates.

Because boxing is a sport of intermittent nature, characterized by short periods of hard effort, it makes sense to do more of this type of running. Furthermore, steady runs will enable you to build a good fitness base, which in turn will help you through your interval running – so the two types are complimentary.

>> Build up gradually

Unless you are already at an intermediate/advanced stage in your boxing fitness program, and running regularly as an integral part of it, you will need to build up your sessions gradually. You will also need to progress them in realistic, achievable ways. If you don't, you risk taking on too much too soon, and may become discouraged or even give up altogether. Here are some guidelines to help get you started.

If you are new to exercise in general, and/or to boxing fitness in particular:

> We advise that you aim to jog for around 20 minutes, once or twice a week. Perhaps you have never run before – so start with a quick stretch (see page 35) and then walk briskly for a little while to warm up.

> Set yourself small targets, such as: power-walk for a minute; jog for a minute; walk slowly for a minute; repeat. This is basic interval training. The details are up to you – the important thing is that you are trying.

> Have some fun – it is possible! Do a bit of punching (up, down, to the front, to the sides, single punches and combinations) as you walk or jog. Walk backward for a bit – always checking behind you for tripping hazards – or "skip" forward and/or sideways. Mix it up. Don't mind how you look to other people, this is about *you*.

When you can complete a 20-minute walk/jog quite comfortably:

> Aim to maintain a gentle run throughout the whole time period. A useful tip here is to bring your speed right down if/when you start to struggle and are tempted to stop. Don't give in to the temptation!

> Keep jogging, no matter how slowly – even if you are almost running on the spot. This isn't any more tiring than a brisk walk, and the first time you manage to keep going for the full 20 minutes it can be a huge psychological boost. Achieve this, and you can consider building two or three such runs into the week, depending on the time you have available.

If you can run steadily for 20 minutes, two or three times a week:

> Now you have a good fitness base and could progress your sessions in a host of different ways. Remember the training variables discussed in chapter 16 on resistance work: these are *duration*, *intensity* and *frequency*.

> You now have the choice of running for longer (duration); running harder (intensity); and/or running more often (frequency). Such variables allow you to mix up your running, literally keeping you on your toes and preventing boredom or staleness from setting in.

>> Keep it up!

Decisions as to where to take your running from here must be made by you. They are likely to be based on a whole range of factors that are individual to your lifestyle, situation and personal preferences – so no one else can dictate your program for you.

The only thing that really matters is that you start to see measurable fitness gains as a direct result of your running sessions. Persevere, because this has to happen. Perhaps you will start to lose weight, or notice that you recover more quickly between rounds of punching bag work in the gym. Such benefits will keep you motivated, so that running may cease to be such an annoyance in your mind.

And if you require further motivation to keep up your running training, keep in mind the "use it or lose it"

principle. It takes a lot of hard work to get from A to B at a run. Don't waste all that effort by allowing laziness to set in, or surmountable obstacles to get in your way. In your head, be the boxer that sets the alarm and heads out into a dark rainy morning. You've come a long way, and we're proud of you.

Running! I hated it at first. As part of my boxing fitness class, which I do with five other ladies, our instructor takes us jogging around the park every Saturday, rain or whine – sorry, shine. In fact, though we love to complain, it's quite fun. We mix up the run by doing some skipping and punching drills, and at the top of the awful hill we stop and do some shadow boxing with a beautiful view. Now I can complete the circuit without getting too out of breath or having to stop. I won't say I look forward to it, but I don't dread it any more. Sometimes I even feel like a boxer.

Helena, 38
Housewife and mom

Appendix: taking it further

Many people find that boxing fitness is sufficiently varied and challenging to keep them motivated in the long term. As we have seen, the training routine is flexible yet easy to structure; it can be used to address a broad range of fitness goals; and it offers the potential for ongoing, measurable progression. Put simply, there is no need to hit anyone, or to get hit, to enjoy and benefit from boxing.

The rise of boxing training today is linked to widespread acknowledgment that in the competitive sport, safety standards have greatly improved. In both its amateur and professional forms, boxing is strictly regulated by the relevant governing bodies, and trainers, managers, promoters and officials are tasked first and foremost with the welfare and fair treatment of every participant.

Perhaps reflecting this, while many people are happy to stay with non-contact boxing, increasing numbers are now interested in taking their training further – into the realms of "sparring" (see below) and even competition. And this interest is not restricted to young people: individuals who are over the age limit (34 years) for an amateur or professional boxing license can engage in competitive boxing via the "white collar" route – a fully regulated form of the sport that welcomes men and women up to the age of 57 into the ring, in an especially safety-conscious environment. See the website of the World White Collar Boxing Association (www.wwcba.org) for more information.

If you are eager to experience boxing in its contact/competitive form, this Appendix will inform you of your options, and guide you to the right places to find the information you need.

Sparring

Sparring is the term applied to a short bout of "practice fighting" between two opponents in a boxing ring. Depending on the aim of the session, it can involve full or restrained contact. *Technical sparring* is undertaken with the intent to perfect a specific drill or movement, rather than to re-create a competitive situation. In the lead-up to a contest, for example, a boxer may study footage of his/her opponent and decide that they are vulnerable to body shots. Sparring sessions would then focus on "working to the body" from different positions, levels and angles, to maximize the boxer's advantage in the upcoming bout.

Conditional sparring is when two participants agree (or the trainer dictates), before the session commences, what is going to happen. For example, it may be determined that one boxer only is to throw punches, while the other rehearses defensive or evasive techniques; or that contact may only be made with light taps or touches by both parties.

Both technical and conditional sparring are great learning tools, not least because working in a "live" situation with another boxer introduces an element of unpredictability – one which cannot be replicated by, for example, the punching bag or focus pads. Taking the example above, you may be practicing working to the body, but (unless otherwise directed) your opponent will be focusing on blocking, slipping

and warding off your shots. Keep trying, and you could find a way through: lesson learned.

In *full-contact sparring*, opponents basically go all out as if they were in a competitive situation. This can give you a good sense of how a fight feels, as you test your body and reactions to the combat experience. However, all-out sparring should be used sparingly, and only by individuals at an advanced level. The pressure of the situation affords little chance of learning new skills, and the likelihood of injury is magnified.

It is paramount that all sparring sessions be closely supervised by a qualified professional, to ensure a safe and controlled environment. For any type of sparring, full personal protective equipment should be worn by both participants: this means headguard, gumshield, groin protector, and sparring gloves of an appropriate weight and quality.

Want to try sparring? Some advice to keep in mind

If you are interested in sparring opportunities, consider the following advice:

1 Because sparring must take place in a ring, under qualified supervision and with full protective equipment, to participate you will need to locate and contact your nearest boxing gym – or find a suitably equipped and staffed health or fitness center. The best way to do this is via the Internet, using Google or another search engine. Look for organizations that seem established and well organized: you can tell a lot from how a website is presented. Compile a list of possible venues.

2 When you have contact details for potentially suitable venues, visit or ring to enquire. Be careful to explain exactly what you are looking for. Don't be offended when they ask you about your weight and your level of fitness/ability/ experience, and answer honestly – it is in both parties' interests. They have to ask, because it is their responsibility to match you with a suitable sparring partner. If you spar with someone a lot heavier, or with someone who is much fitter or technically advanced, you may become discouraged and/or injured; the venue's reputation will also be placed in jeopardy. Remember to ask your own questions, too: who will be supervising the sessions, what do they cost, and do they provide equipment or should you purchase your own?

③ If you find what looks like a good set-up, great – show up and enjoy it. But always keep in mind that any type of glove-to-body contact involves an element of risk. This can be minimized if each participant respects their sparring partner, adheres to any pre-agreed conditions, and keeps their temper in check at all times. If you try and aren't happy with the situation at that venue, don't think twice about leaving and looking for another. Pride doesn't, and mustn't, come into it.

④ Whatever type of sparring you engage in, make no mistake – it is very hard work. Even if you are at an advanced stage in your boxing fitness program, the day after your first sparring session you will discover muscles you never knew you had! You may also gain a few minor bruises, but there is no reason for you to suffer anything more serious. Again, if things seem too "full on" for you, talk to the trainer – or look elsewhere.

Competition

If you'd like to compete in the sport of boxing, you have three avenues open to you: amateur boxing; professional boxing; or white collar boxing (discussed above).

Amateur boxing

As the name suggests, amateur boxers do not compete for financial gain. The sport is conducted in schools and universities/colleges, at the Olympics (since 1920) and Commonwealth Games (since 1930), and in other venues as sanctioned by the various arms of the sport's governing body – the International Amateur Boxing Association (AIBA). The AIBA website www.aiba.org provides news, events information, and documentation pertaining

to the sport of amateur boxing, as well as contact details for and links to national federations and regional/local subdivisions.

The minimum age for competitive amateur boxing is 11 years, and the maximum, 34 years. To be eligible to fight, all boxers must have a full medical; if they are pronounced fit, then they are given official clearance (known as being "carded").

Like professional boxers (see below), amateurs compete in weight divisions to ensure their safety and welfare – since, generally speaking, the heavier the individual, the more powerful the punch. The lightest division is the "Light Flyweight," at 48 kg; the heaviest is the "Super Heavyweight," where fighters weigh in at more than 91 kg. As a further safety measure, below the age of 17 (when they are known as Juniors) amateur boxers cannot concede more than 12 months in age to their opponent.

Unlike professional boxers, who fight bare-chested and with no protective headgear, amateur boxers wear blue or red singlets (to demonstrate which "corner" they belong in) and headguards are mandatory. Their gloves weigh 10 ounces and have a white strip on the main hitting area around the knuckles. Scoring is by "points": for a boxer to score a point, they must hit the head or body (above the belt) of their opponent with the knuckle part of the glove. Five judges sit ringside, each with a computer scoring button to press for each boxer, and three of the five must hit their button within one second of each other for the point to register. The winner of a bout is the fighter with the most points, unless the referee stops the bout before the final bell. Rounds are usually two minutes long, with four rounds generally making up an amateur contest.

If you would like to try amateur boxing, your first port of call might be your local boxing club or gym; they will show you the set-up, and talk to you about training and competitive opportunities. Alternatively, contact the United States Amateur Boxing organization [USAB] – www.usaboxing.org). They will give you contact details for your regional subdivision, who in turn can advise you as to first steps, and provide a list of suitable clubs in your area for you to get in touch with.

Professional boxing

Professional boxers fight for a fee, known as a "purse," which is shared with their trainer and manager. In championships, they compete for a title in their weight division: for example, Clinton was British, Commonwealth and European Light Welterweight Champion. The title is accompanied by a trophy consisting of an elaborately ornate belt, which has to be defended by or won from the boxer – together with their coveted title.

Professional bouts are longer than amateur bouts, typically ranging from 10 to 12 three-minute rounds. Three judges sit ringside, and there is a referee in the ring throughout. If the fight "goes the distance" – in other words, is not stopped before the end – the winner will be chosen based on points (i.e. according to how many rounds the judges think a boxer has won).

The referee can stop the fight at any time if he believes that one participant is unable to defend themselves; this is known as a "technical knockout" (TKO). A TKO may also be awarded against a boxer if they simply stop fighting or if their "corner" stops the contest by literally "throwing in the towel." And a "knockout?" When a boxer simply cannot rise from the canvas, sufficiently recovered from the blow that felled them, to satisfy the referee that it is safe for them to continue.

Because injury is much more likely in professional than in amateur boxing, the licensing process is more demanding. To be eligible to fight professionally, you must first sign a contract with a professional boxing trainer and manager, who will endorse your application to the relevant Board of Boxing Control. You will then be interviewed, and if the Board is satisfied, it may make an appointment to watch you spar. If your sparring session is approved, you must then undergo a stringent medical test, which includes a sight test and an MRI scan.

If you are interested in boxing for a living, your best bet is first to contact your country's Board of Boxing Control; they will put you in touch with the appropriate Area Council, which will advise you from there. It's a tough career choice, and not one to be taken lightly! But as you may already be finding from your boxing fitness program – boxing is an alluring world.

Good luck – and *hands up*!

Resources

>> Clothing and equipment

Boxing equipment and apparel is now available from a wide range of online stores. Here we provide a small selection of tried-and-tested suppliers, but feel free to research your own. The following is a list of sites that will ship internationally:

> www.everlast.com

> www.balazsboxing.com

> www.boxingequipmentusa.com

> www.yorkbarbell.com

> www.lonsdaleusa.com

> www.boxingequipmentus.com/index.php

At the time of writing, Everlast – an iconic boxing brand – will only ship within the US from its dedicated website www.everlast.com. However, Everlast equipment can be ordered via Amazon and other large online stores, and you are likely to find plenty in your local sports stores.

Many elite boxers have now created their own branded merchandise, which is available via their websites. Among these, try:

> www.brandhatton.com (Ricky Hatton, former world champion, Light Welterweight division)

> www.goldenboystore.com (Oscar De La Hoya, ten times world champion in six weight divisions)

> www.hayemaker.com (David Haye, WBA World Heavyweight Champion at the time of writing)

> www.floydmayweather.com (Floyd Mayweather, five-division world champion)

> www.amirkhanshop.com (Amir Khan, WBA World Super Lightweight Champion at the time of writing)

> www.klitschko.com (the Klitschko brothers – between them, holding every world title in the Heavyweight division, with the exception of the WBA)

Adidas now manufactures some excellent boxing gear, which you can explore via the links at www.adidas.com. And for the *crème-de-la-crème* of boxing clothing and equipment, dream about stepping into the ring geared up head-to-toe in Cleto Reyes: www.cletoreyes.com.

>> Governing bodies

Amateur boxing

www.aiba.org The International Boxing Association, originally the *Association Internationale de Boxe Amateur* and still referred to as the AIBA. Sanctions amateur boxing matches, and awards world and subordinate championships.

www.usaboxing.org The official website of USA Boxing – the national governing body for amateur boxing in America.

www.canadianboxing.com The Canadian Boxing Federation. The site includes tournament dates, online newsletter, rules, history and lists of all recent tournament results.

www.abae.co.uk The Amateur Boxing Association of England (ABAE). As a national governing body, the ABAE is responsible for administering, developing and promoting amateur boxing throughout England.

www.goldengloves.com This program leads the way in promoting amateur boxing in the States, and produces many competitors for America's boxing teams in the Pan-Am and Olympic Games.

Professional boxing

Note: Professional boxing has a number of governing bodies, each sanctioning different contests and awarding different championship titles. This can be confusing, as it may lead to the existence of multiple world champions in any weight division. Below are the three main organizations: websites include brief histories, fighter rankings, schedules, results, a list of current champions, federation by-laws, and rules and regulations.

www.wbaonline.com The World Boxing Association (WBA) – professional boxing's oldest governing body, founded in 1921.

www.wbcboxing.com The World Boxing Council (WBC), established in 1963.

www.ibf-usba-boxing.com The International Boxing Federation (IBF).

In Great Britain, the governing body for professional boxing is the British Boxing Board of Control (BBBofC) www.bbbofc.com. For the rest of Europe, visit www.boxebu.com and follow the links.

In America no single, unified governing body exists; individual state-controlled commissions have different sets of standards, rules and guidelines. For a list of the commissions plus links, go to www.ringsidebygus.com.

White collar boxing

A form of competitive boxing which allows people who have taken up the sport later in life, or who fall outside the 34-year-old maximum age limit for amateur and professional boxing, to participate in a competitive environment with added safety measures.

Its umbrella governing body is the World White Collar Boxing Association, and the website www.wwcba.org gives information and membership details for competitors, training establishments, trainers/coaches, events and promotions, and officials.

Glossary

Adaptation – see *fitness*.

Amateur boxing – the non-professional form of the sport, regulated by the International Boxing Association (AIBA). Participants wear protective headgear, and gloves which have a white portion over the knuckle. Scoring is based on the number of clean punches delivered with the white part of the glove. Amateur boxing is practiced in schools and colleges, at the Olympic and Commonwealth Games, and elsewhere as sanctioned by the relevant national or regional governing bodies.

Bag gloves – a type of boxing glove worn for any type of punching that involves no contact with another person (for example, when hitting the *punching bag*, *speed ball* or *focus pads*). Bag gloves are lighter than *sparring gloves*; they have a free-moving rather than a stitched thumb, and are loose rather than bound or laced at the wrist/lower arm.

Bandages – see *hand-wraps*.

Belt – refers to that part of a boxer's body above which it is legal to deliver *body shots*. A punch delivered "below the belt" is not permitted and will be penalized. Ornate belts are traditionally awarded to professional boxing champions by way of trophies.

Bobbing and weaving – see *defensive/evasive techniques*.

Body composition – an element of *fitness* which refers to how much of the body is made up of fat (expressed as "body fat percentage"), and how much consists of lean tissue (muscle, bone, tendons and ligaments).

Body fat percentage – see *body composition*.

Body Mass Index (BMI) – a scale used to determine whether a person is at a healthy weight, or is overweight ("obese"). The BMI is calculated using measures of weight and height, and does not take account of *body composition* or natural body type/build.

Body shot – a punch to an opponent's body. Body shots are allowed to the front and sides of the body, in the area above the waist or *belt*.

Bout – another name for a boxing contest. When professional boxers fight for a championship title (e.g. Heavyweight Champion of the World), the bouts are 12 *rounds* long. Amateur bouts vary in the number of rounds, which may be fought over two or three minutes.

Boxing clock – a special clock which indicates the passage of *rounds* and rest (*recovery*) periods, via a bell or other electronic signal.

Boxing ring – the "ring" is actually a square, consisting of a raised platform covered with padding and a durable canvas. There is a post at each corner, to which are fixed four parallel rows of ropes; these form a flexible, continuous barrier that prevents boxers from falling off the platform. Fighters also use the ropes to lean against, enabling them to rest or fight defensively or strategically.

Combinations – groups or sequences of punches, as opposed to individual shots (see *jab*, *cross*, *hook*, *uppercut*).

Compound exercises – those resistance exercises (see *resistance training*) which involve more than one joint, and thus work several muscles or muscle groups at the same time. See also *isolation exercises*.

Core training – also known as "core strength," or "core stability." The core consists of all the muscles that stabilize, align and move the trunk of the body. These muscles are not limited to the "six-pack," but also include the deeper internal muscles which help us maintain stability in motion.

Counter – see *counterpunch*.

Counterpunch – also known as a "counter." A shot delivered in direct response to a punch received.

Cross – also known as the "straight right" (from an *orthodox stance*). The cross is delivered with the back hand, across the body, and is accompanied by a pivot of the hips and shoulders to achieve power.

Cross-overs – an advanced skipping technique where the arms are crossed at the elbows on the downward arc of the rope.

Defensive/evasive techniques – ways in which a boxer will dodge, block or ward off ("parry") an opponent's punches. Ducking, slipping, and bobbing and weaving are such techniques.

Double-unders – an advanced skipping technique which makes two turns of the rope for each double-footed jump.

Ducking – see *defensive/evasive techniques*.

Duration – see *training variables*.

Dynamic stretching – used primarily as a warm-up, this involves sport-specific movements to prepare the body for the particular kind of exercise to follow. See also *static stretching*.

Fitness – all the different qualities that can be improved and enhanced through exercise. The term usually is applied to physical qualities, such as strength, speed and stamina, but can also encompass emotional and/or psychological elements (e.g. confidence and a sense of well-being). Fitness gains are achieved through a process of overload and adaptation, whereby we challenge the body by making it work harder, so that it can adapt to undertake the same task more efficiently next time around.

Focus pads – padded, hand-held "mitts" of varying size and design used by suitably trained practitioners. The pads are held and moved in different positions, and at different ranges and angles, so that individual punches and *combinations* can be rehearsed.

Frequency – see *training variables*.

Groin protector – personal protective equipment worn by both amateur and professional boxers.

Guard – the classic "hands up" position of a boxer. A correct guard not only protects the jaw and chin, but also provides the best position from which to deliver a technically sound and effective punch or *combination*.

Gumshield – also known as a mouthguard. Worn to protect a boxer's mouth and teeth from damage caused by blows to the chin and jaw, a gumshield is mandatory in both amateur and professional contests, and should also be worn by anyone undertaking *sparring*.

Hand-wraps – also referred to as "bandages." Lengths of cotton or elastic-type material used to "wrap" the hands before putting on gloves for training or competition. Hand-wraps prevent the skin of the hands from chafing, and protect the small bones of the hands and wrist from potential damage caused by punching.

Headguard – a type of "helmet" worn for *sparring* and for *amateur boxing* contests, designed to protect the face and head from damage caused by punches. Professional boxers do not wear protective headgear.

Heavy bag – see *punch bag*.

Hook – a semi-circular punch, designed for delivery with the lead (front) hand to the side of an opponent's head or chin.

Intensity – see *training variables*.

Interval training – involves working relatively hard for a specified period of time, followed by a defined rest (*recovery*) period, followed by repetition of the hard effort, and so on. By definition, boxing training is interval training, since it is performed over set effort periods (*rounds*) followed by periods of one minute's recovery.

Isolation exercises – those resistance exercises (see *resistance training*) which involve a single joint, and thus work one muscle or muscle group at a time. See also *compound exercises*.

Jab – the most important punch in a boxer's repertoire, delivered with the lead (front) hand straight out from the shoulder.

Neutral spine – refers to the natural curvature made by the backbone, which if correctly aligned forms a gentle "S" shape when viewed from the side. Keeping a neutral spine is an important part of good posture and exercise technique.

One-two – the term for a *jab* followed by a *cross*.

Orthodox – see *stance*.

Overload – see *fitness*.

Prizefighting – also known as "fisticuffs," "pugilism" and "bare-knuckle fighting." A *bout* or contest between two unarmed individuals, who wear no gloves or other kind of protection.

Professional boxing – as the name suggests, boxers fight for a fee (see *purse*). Professional fighters wear no *headguard*; *bouts* are scored by "decision" made by a referee and/or judges sitting ringside.

Pulse-raiser – that initial part of the warm-up which involves a few minutes of light exercise to raise the heart rate, lubricate the joints, and increase muscle elasticity.

Punching bag – sometimes referred to as a *heavy bag*. A type of padded "bag" used for practicing punching, by providing a cushioned resistance to individual shots and *combinations*. There are a number of different types of punching bags available: see also *speed ball*.

Purse – the money collected by a professional boxer after a *bout*, to be shared with their manager and trainer.

Queensberry Rules – introduced in 1867 under the patronage of the Marquess of Queensberry, these 12 rules regulated the sport of *prizefighting*, and established (among other controls) the use of a roped-off *ring*, three-minute *rounds*, and padded gloves for the protection of both combatants.

Reach – the range of a punch. If a boxer has relatively long arms, he or she is said to have "good natural reach."

Recovery – basically, a period of rest. In boxing, each *round* of effort is followed by a recovery period of one-minute's duration.

Repetition – when applied to *core training*, *resistance training* or *roadwork* intervals, a repetition is a single, complete effort or exercise that may be repeated any number of times.

Resistance training – training during which you overload your muscles by making them work against an opposing force (resistance) such as gravity, a weight (e.g. a dumbbell), or your own bodyweight.

Roadwork – running. Boxers run to increase their stamina, which in turn facilitates *recovery* between *rounds* of training, *sparring* and competition.

Rounds – intervals of training or competitive effort. Professional boxers train and compete over three-minute rounds; in amateur boxing, rounds may be two or three minutes long.

Set – when applied to *core training*, *resistance training* or *roadwork* intervals, a set is a group of *repetitions* performed continuously without stopping. Each set is usually followed by a specific period of rest (*recovery*).

Shadow boxing – a form of boxing training which involves pitting yourself against an imaginary opponent. If you shadow box facing a mirror, you can be your own opponent, and practice all your shots, *combinations*, footwork and *defensive/evasive techniques*.

Sideways-on – in the correct *stance*, the body should be positioned slightly sideways (rather than "square-on") to an opponent, with the front foot, hip and shoulders in line. This minimizes the area exposed to a potential *body shot*; maximizes *reach*; and allows twisting from the hips and shoulders to make a punch more powerful and effective.

Slipping – see *defensive/evasive techniques*.

Southpaw – see *stance*.

Sparring – the term used to describe "practice fighting" between two individuals in the ring. Because there is contact involved, both participants must wear suitable personal protective equipment (see *headguard*, *groin protector*, *gumshield*, and the Appendix).

Sparring gloves – a type of boxing glove worn for any type of punching that involves contact with another person (see also *sparring*). Sparring gloves are more substantial and padded than *bag gloves*; they extend and fasten further up the wrist/lower arm; and have the thumb stitched to the body of the glove.

Speed bag – a small, air-filled *punching bag* anchored to a "rebound platform" that is mounted parallel to the ground. The ball is used to improve speed and hand–eye co-ordination.

Square-on – see *sideways-on*.

Stance – how to stand when boxing. The stance may be with the left foot in front, known as "orthodox," or with the right foot in front, known as "southpaw." Depending on his or her preferred stance, a boxer may also be known as an orthodox or a southpaw fighter.

Static stretching – part of the warm-up and/or cool-down, this type of stretching involves slowly reaching a point of tension in the muscle(s) of the targeted area. The position is then held for 10-15 seconds, before relaxing out of the stretch. See also *dynamic stretching*.

Training variables – ways in which you can vary your training efforts to achieve particular *fitness* gains. These include duration (the time period over which you perform an exercise or activity); intensity (how hard you are working in an exercise or activity); and frequency (how often you perform an exercise or activity). See also *interval training*.

Uppercut – a "vertical" punch, thrown up towards the target, which may be an opponent's chin or body.

White-collar boxing – a fully regulated form of boxing open to men and women aged 25 to 57, allowing those who do not hold an amateur or professional licence to get into the ring in a competitive environment with added safety measures.

Index

overload and adaptation 16–17, 92, 148, 150
    see also fitness

rounds 17, 29, 104, 169g
running 158–60

p

partners, training 19
patience 74, 85, 101
personal trainers 19–20, 96
posture 36, 140
power 14, 73
pregnancy 98
prizefighting 7, 169g
professional boxing 7, 29, 164, 169g
    governing bodies 166
protein 79, 81–2
pulse-raisers 35, 169g
punch bags 30–2, 70–3, 169g
punches 48–55, 56–7
    counter- 63
purse, boxers' 7, 164, 169g
push-ups 155

q

Queensbury Rules 7, 169g
questionnaires ('PAR-Qs') 96–7

r

reach 47, 169g
record keeping 104–6, 140–1
recovery time 104, 169g
relaxin 98
repetitions 141, 169g
resistance training 148–57, 169g
resources 165–6
RICE (rest, ice, compression, elevation) 91
rings, boxing 32–3, 167g
roadwork 158–60, 169g

s

safety 1, 3, 10, 78, 88, 101
    hand-wrapping 27, 88
    skipping 66
saturated fats 83
sets 141, 169g
shadow boxing 64–5, 104, 169–70g
shoulder presses 154
side lunges 154
side planks 145
sideways-on 25, 47, 53, 170g
sit-ups 142
skipping 60, 66–9, 92
skipping ropes 22–3, *28*
slipping 62
soft tissue injury 91
southpaws 46–50, *52*, 170g
sparring 161–3, 170g
sparring gloves *28*, 30, 71, 88, 162, 170g
speed 14, 73
speed ball 73–4, 170g
split squats 153
split-leg squat thrusts 135
square on 25, 47, 58
squat thrusts 134
squats
    basic bodyweight 152
    directional squat jumps 136
    duck 153
    split 153
    split-leg squat thrusts 135
    squat thrusts 134
stance 25, 45–8, 53, 58, 170g
star jumps 133
static stretching 36, 37–40, 170g
straight/tuck jumps 133
stress 8–9
stretching 35–6
    exercises 37–42
Swiss balls 33, 141–2
    exercises 146–7, 152

t

techniques 89–91
training sessions 103–7
    advanced level 118–24
    boxing circuits 107, 129–36
    intermediate level 114–17
    with minimum equipment 125–7
    novice level 108–13
    planning 15–20
    in various locations 128
    see also clothing; equipment
training variables 150, 170g
triceps dips 155

u

unsaturated oils 83
uppercuts 51–2, 57, 170g

v

vertical leg abdominal crunches 143
vitamins 80, 83

w

warm-ups 35–42, 65, 89, 96
weight loss 80, 83
    and exercise 84–5
weights 33
    and young adults 95
    see also resistance training
white collar boxing 10, 166, 170g
women 8, 60, 96, 98

y

young adults, and boxing fitness 93–5